POETS ON THE ROAD

Poets on the Road

Maureen Owen

&

Barbara Henning

First edition

Published by City Point Press
www.citypointpress.com

For sales inquiries, contact Simon & Schuster (866) 506-1949
For rights inquiries, contact City Point Press (203) 571-0871
For author inquiries, contact Barbara at www.facebook.com/barbara.henning
        contact Maureen at www.facebook.com/maureen.owen.399

Paperback ISBN: 978-1-947951-70-9
eBook ISBN: 978-1-947951-71-6

Cover photo by Val Wilkes, owner of Rocket Inn
Cover photo of open road by Maureen Owen
Drawing on title page of Maureen by Yvonne Jacquette and of Barbara by Rie Shimamura
Book design by HR Hegnauer

Manufactured in the United States of America

TABLE OF CONTENTS

*Throughout the book, bolded names and words indicate links in the ebook and are listed in Appendix C of the printed book. All links were active at the time of publication. Links to reading series and venues are under "Appendix B: Agenda."

INTRODUCTION
POETRY ODYSSEY IN A HONDA

In the final days of February and early into March of 2019, as an atmospheric river stretched from Hawaii to the North Coast of California bringing with it enough rain to swell the Russian River to flood levels not seen since 1995, two intrepid poets, Maureen Owen and Barbara Henning, drove up from Southern California for a scheduled reading at Moe's Bookstore in Berkeley, and then on to the final stop on the West Coast of their cross country reading tour at North Bay Letterpress Arts in Sebastopol, California.

Maureen and Barbara had put their ambitious plan for a cross country poetry reading tour into motion a year earlier by lining up dates and venues that would take them from Brooklyn, where Barbara lives, to Denver two months later, where Maureen makes her home. Their venues would include upscale bookstores, coffee houses, museums, legendary used bookstores, botanical gardens, university classrooms, art centers, and artist coops—in short, a unique sampling of poetry environments tracing an arc across the Southern States, the Southwest, and up the West Coast before hooking back to the Rockies.

Framed as a personal challenge, the poets hit the road much in the manner of itinerant preachers and musicians, lodging at discount motels, funky hostels, Airbnbs, and with friends along the way. Adding a social media touch, Maureen and Barbara created a blog of their tour so that friends, family, hosts, and fellow poets might also share in their adventure.

Their starting point on a wintery 18th of January Friday night was the Belladonna Readings Series at the Jackson McNally Bookstore in the trendy Williamsburg neighborhood of Brooklyn. A standout crowd of New York literati came to see them off. Two days and two hundred and fifty miles later, the poets found themselves in Washington, DC, for an afternoon reading with Terrence Winch and Erica Howsare at the DC Arts Center. Their next stop was in Pensacola, Florida, for a reading the following Saturday, the 26th, at the Pensacola Museum of Art which allowed them to take their time and enjoy a leisurely thousand-mile drive through the much warmer South and appreciate the bucolic landscapes of backroad America. From Pensacola it was on to Mobile, Alabama, and a reading at the Mobile Botanical Gardens the following day, the 27th, and then New Orleans for a Wednesday night reading at the Dragonfly Poetry and Performance Ritual Space on the 30th. At this pace, the poets were averaging a reading every two and half days and had traveled, accounting for stops and detours, easily fifteen hundred miles.

Although a road trip across North American calls to mind Jack Kerouac's youthful meanderings of self-discovery, this reading tour was more in the manner of Bashō's late life journeys through the backcountry of Japan. Both poets, now in their seventies, have made poetry the focus of most of their adult lives. The road trip was in a sense a pilgrimage of reengagement with their calling as poets, and a chance to reacquaint themselves with like-minded friends, old and new, in a far-flung landscape of American poetry.

Feb 2nd, Groundhog Day and James Joyce's birthday, found the poets in Austin at the hub of Texas literary culture and a well-attended reading at Malvern Books with local poet Ashley Smith Keyfitz joining them at the mic. From there it was on to their next gig, a seven-hundred-mile trek to Albuquerque for a Feb 7th reading at Bookworks that included a side trip to the Buddy Holly Museum in Lubbock, Texas. Tucson, Arizona, awaited them for their reading at the Steinfeld Warehouse Community Arts Center on February 16th after an overnight stay at the unique Rocket Inn in Truth Or Consequences, New Mexico.

By now the travelers were coming to terms with the vast and empty distances of the West. They logged 150 miles from Albuquerque to Truth Or Consequences and another three hundred miles to Tucson, Barbara's old stomping grounds. There the poets took a much-needed breather to enjoy the familiar sights and reconnect with old friends before heading for California, and the beginning of their sprint north up the coast the following week.

All the while the poets were making their way west, California was experiencing one of the wettest winters in decades. The month of January saw one storm system after another batter the West Coast with saturating rain. It was under those conditions the poets arrived in Southern California in mid-February. By then they'd been on the road over a month.

On Thursday night, the 21st, scheduled to read to Professor Mark Wallace's "The Community and World" series, Barbara navigated her eleven-year-old Honda through the blinding rain and hail on a swamped expressway looking for the exit to the state university in San Marcos. It was their welcome to winter in California. The following evening, on the tail end of the storm, but still dark and blustery, the poets headed to La Jolla and their gig at the legendary D.G. Wills Used Bookstore.

Their arrival in Venice was on Sunday where that afternoon Maureen and Barbara read at the renowned Beyond Baroque. The poets then headed north for a four-hundred-mile drive to San Francisco and the Bay Area on February 25th. The predicted rainfall for some parts of Northern California was upward of a foot and half in the next few days. Based on calculations of the amount of rain, the local rivers would exceed their banks.

Staying at an Airbnb in Berkeley, Barbara and Maureen got a taste of Bay Area traffic congestion while traveling to visit Diane di Prima at the Jewish Home for the Aged in San Francisco. To the north of them flooding and an evacuation order was in effect for those in the path of the rising waters. It was a cause for concern as their next stop after Berkeley was Monte Rio, a little hamlet on the Russian River, where I have lived since 1973.

On Thursday, the 28th, the poets once again travelled to San Francisco for a reading in Steve Dickison's class at San Francisco State University. Then it was back across the Bay Bridge to the celebrated Moe's Bookstore for an evening reading attended by a select group of East Bay literati. By then the Russian River had crested at 45.4 feet and was slowly but surely retreating to nonthreatening levels.

The next day Maureen and Barbara's arrival in the North Bay was fraught with the high drama of a post flood region under evacuation order. As the flood waters receded, county officials scrambled to assess the damage and limit access in an effort to thwart the potential for looting and the inevitable crisis tourism. As it turned out, the restrictions were rescinded by midday and the poets easily accomplished the remainder of their journey without encountering any checkpoints.

A somewhat soggy Sunday March 3rd afternoon brought Barbara and Maureen to their next venue, North Bay Letterpress Arts in Sebastopol. NBLA is a unique collective of a dozen or so print artists and poets dedicated to the craft of letterpress printing. The poets were greeted by a lively audience of working artists, friends, including Sandy Berrigan who had traveled all the way down from Albion on the Mendocino coast for the occasion, and, in Maureen's case, relatives. Despite the recent disaster affecting so many of their lives they were delighted to be in attendance. The reading and the subsequent social engagement with the poets might be considered as a kind of "flood relief." As an added bonus, Eric Johnson, then director of NBLA, handset and printed poem cards by each of the poets to commemorate the occasion.

On Monday, the 5th, the poets hooked south and on to Mojave to avoid having to go east through the snowbound Sierras. From there it was another determined jog to Santa Fe, and then the last leg of travel, arriving in Denver on the 8th. By then their epic journey had added about 5,550 miles to the odometer of Barbara's trusty Honda Fit. On Tuesday, March 19th, almost two months to the day of their departure, Maureen Owen and Barbara Henning, joined by poet Crisosto Apache, held their final reading of their cross-country tour at the Mercury Café's F Bomb Series in Denver. With it, they brought closure to one of the great poetry odysseys of modern times.

— Pat Nolan
Monte Rio, 2022

BROOKLYN
JANUARY 16 - 19, 2019

In January of 2018, Maureen and I started imagining a poetry reading road trip. She was preparing to retire, and I thought I could swing a trip if I sublet my apartment. One year later, after lots of phone calls, emails, and much planning, Maureen took a train from Denver, the Amtrak *California Zephyr*, and she arrived in Brooklyn at my apartment in a cab on Wednesday, the 16th of January. (Barb)

❀

Through Iowa snowy farm fields with Black Angus pop outs. A single black steer, way out in the middle of frozen cornstalks poking through the snow. In Mendota, Illinois, silos on the edge of town. All snow around. Huge ear of corn painted on the whole side of one, open eared, sun bright yellow kernels with sprightly green husks curled up the sides. Then a snowplow buried in the snow. At night around Lake Michigan and then following Lake Erie. Arriving in Buffalo at daylight, torn snow, somber mauve landscape, the frozen forests of upper NY State.

Coming down the Hudson toward NYC, smoky graphite clouds ripped apart by dayglow orange horizon.

Train delayed and slowed by the river rescue patrol. Hoping no one is drowning. *The Lakeshore Limited* in beauty follows the Hudson, river frozen over with big chunks of ice pushing against the shore. Unfortunately, it does not have a dining car so arriving famished. (MO)

❊

While Maureen was coasting along on the *California Zephyr* and *The Lakeshore Limited*, I was packing up my apartment for a subletter, packing books, running errands to buy this and that for the trip, responding to online students, trying to clear a spot in my little studio for a blow-up bed for Maureen to sleep on. We quickly discovered we both like chilling out watching British detective films, last night, *Poirot*. (Barb)

❊

Our first reading will be tomorrow, Friday, Jan. 18th, at McNally Jackson Books in Williamsburg, Brooklyn, 76 N 4th Street, at 7 p.m., a Belladonna reading.

Jan. 18, 2022. For both of us, this was a fabulous gala launch. Thanks to Belladonna and those at McNally Jackson Books in Williamsburg. Special thanks to Rachael Wilson for organizing, curating, and making lovely broadsides.

We were especially happy that Pamela Lawton displayed the original artwork for the cover of our pamphlet, *Poets on the Road*, and she spoke about her process in making the covers. (See Appendix B for poems originally included in the pamphlet.) She described the first time she ever made a cover for a poet was for a book by Lewis Warsh; she blew up lines from one of his poems and hung them around her studio; then she lived with those for a while and then began painting. She mentioned how she originally became connected to our poetic community through her relationship with the poet Elio Schneeman. Here is a photo her partner, Danny Licul, took at the event of Pamela and the books:

Some of those who attended were Ed Friedman, Patricia Spears Jones, Joel Lewis, Sandy Flitterman-Lewis, Cheryl Fish, Lydia Cortez, James Polk, Sally Young, Cliff Fyman, Peter Bushyeager, Greg Masters, Hillary Keel, Christina Kelleger, Danny Licul, Phyllis Wat, Lewis Warsh, Jen Firestone, Toni Simon, Joanna Furman, James Loop, Elinor Nauen, Evelyn Reilly, Micah Saperstein, Rie Shimamura, KB Nemcosky, Jim Feast, Esther Hyneman, John Godfrey, Mark Nasdor, Ryan Nowlin, Judi and Bob Dumont and Annabelle Levitt. Special thanks to Rie Shimamura for designing our blog and Barbara's son Michah Saperstein for photographing. (Barb/MO)

See Appendix C for a link to a recording of our BELLADONNA READING.

Left: Cam from McNally Jackson and Rachael Wilson. Right: Crowd photo of Ryan Nowlin, Lewis Warsh and Ed Friedman. *Photos by Michah Saperstein*

Barbara's son, Michah Saperstein and Rie Shimamura

Maureen and Barbara.
Photos by James Loop

With a Bang

—with a bang—the hairy flower wild petunia—flings its tiny
seeds—sudden and far—how and why—the scientist—kneels
down—clamps a metal band—on a pigeon's leg—her initials—
and id number—my broken toe—x-rayed, recorded—at the
Bleecker Street station—an old man—with head bowed—
kneeling—on cardboard—an over crowded—shopping cart—
a sign—*repent—the end is near*—the Indian guru whispers—
the only sin—to harm oneself—to harm another—is to harm
oneself—to repent too much—is to harm oneself—on the
platform—the next generation—leans over a keyboard—riffs,
breaks, runs—his body hunched—fingers flying—30 miles
an hour—all at once—released—the seeds spin outward—
the bird flutters into the air—   *(18 Mar 2018)*

—Barbara Henning

Printed on the occasion of her Belladonna* reading with Maureen Owen at McNally
Jackson bookstore in Williamsburg on Friday, January 18, 2019, and in commemoration
of their road trip reading tour, "Poets on the Road."

"the queen is a triangle
the knight is a right angle
the bishop diagonal

moving   the pawn is like the queen
only lesser"   she said

the pines look wooly   up November's air
She rolls her hand in crisp leaves
under her chair
What are you looking for?
My glove
You have both your gloves on
Oh   I thought   I dropped one

—Maureen Owen

Printed on the occasion of her Belladonna* reading with Barbara Henning at
McNally Jackson bookstore in Williamsburg on Friday, January 18, 2019,
and in commemoration of their road trip reading tour, "Poets on the Road."

Belladonna broadsides by Rachel Wilson

Washington DC & Beyond

January 19 - 22, 2019

The next morning, on January 19, 2019, we were flying along in Barbara's Honda, leaving Brooklyn, on the first leg of our reading road tour, headed for DC to our next reading at the **"In Your Ear Poetry Reading Series."** Along the way we chatted as we motored above bodies of water on the Verrazano Narrows Bridge over Lower New York Bay. (MO)

❀

In the morning, my son, Michah, helped us load the car. As we drove toward DC, we talked about our families, losses, our archives, #MeToo, Charlie Rose, Al Franken, Kevin Spacey. After crossing several rivers, we started talking about experiences with rape, Maureen fighting off attackers, me once trapped and then another time running. As we passed through New Jersey, the landscape was desolate in a winter dry way. I looked up and a flock of geese passed overhead. Maybe they were heading south, like us. (Barb)

❀

We stayed with the wonderful Irish poet and story writer, **Terence Winch** and his wife, **Susan Campbell**, in Silver Springs, Maryland. Susan is a painter and has done numerous book covers. Among them a gorgeously mysterious cover for Terence's title, *Falling Out of Bed in a Room with No Floor,* and an entire book on the poet Doug Lang. Inside the stunning cover the pages run wild with collage, text, paintings, quotes, and photographs. Our accommodations in their house were spectacular, including a sudden appearance of Beckett staring down from the medicine cabinet in the bathroom. (MO)

❀

The mess of travelling, coupled with exhaustion, sometimes created chaos and confusion. Tired of driving and fumbling around with some things, I got out of the car at Terence's house and said to Maureen, "I guess we should lock the door." Then we went into the house and met everyone. As we were all getting ready to go out to the car to bring things in, I looked in my bag, no keys. "Oh, shit I locked the keys in the car." We laughed and called GEICO for road service. We talked for an hour and then the guy from GEICO was spotted in the driveway, walking around the car with a yellow stick. He opened a passenger door. I went out to give him the tip we had promised if he would come quickly. And he said, "I don't understand what the problem is. All the doors were unlocked!"

Our reading took place on Sunday, January 20th, at 3 p.m. at the DC Arts Center. Terence and Erika Howsare read with us and the evening soared. Terence's first poem was about his mother. Earlier in the kitchen, he had talked about how his mother died when he was sixteen and his father when Terence was twenty-seven. Those losses reverberate in his light-hearted poems. He often pokes fun at himself in a light poetic way. While he was reading a poem, entitled "Poor Country," about a virus that we think shut down the hospitals, suddenly a bunch of noisy theater people drifted through our space to use the bathroom. Terence stopped reading and said, "It's all the fault of the people on the bathroom line." And then everyone laughed. (Barb)

❀

It was a special audience of poets and friends. Some of those we knew in-cluded: K. Lorraine Graham, Constance McKenna, Doug Lang, Heather Grant, Rod Smith, Simon Schuchat, David Beaudouin, Bevil Townsend, and Indran Amirthanayagam.

Books, crowd photo, Simon Schuchat and Maureen (Barb); Chris Mason and David Beaudouin *(MO)*

After a bite to eat we went to Petworth Citizen where Terence played the accordion and his son Michael played fiddle in their monthly Irish Traditional Music Session. We all felt like dancing the Irish jig. (MO)

✤

It was exhilarating to hear Terence, his son Michael, and others play impromptu Irish music in a session at a long table of musicians in the bar. At one point, I called my son, Mook, on FaceTime so he could see and hear them. I took a few shots of Terence playing the box and his son on the fiddle. When I sent him a copy of the below photo, he wrote back, "Thanks for the photo. Playing music with Michael—my favorite thing to do in life." One story he told at the kitchen table was about playing music in the White House when Clinton was president; this took place after Clinton had resolved some conflict in Ireland. (Barb)

Terence and Michael Winch *(Barb)*

The next morning: Terence taped Maureen and me reading poems for his **"Best American Poetry Blog."** Maureen read a poem dedicated to Ed Friedman and I read "Here We Are" from *A Day Like Today*. (Barb)

❀

We left DC in howling winds and unseasonable biting cold after Terence made an incredible Irish breakfast of scrambled eggs, bacon, crusty, buttery toast, and much tea and coffee. Delicious! I asked him if he remembered making just such a breakfast for me many years ago when, as a young poet, I first came to DC to give a reading. One never forgets an Irish breakfast by Terence. (MO)

❀

As we were getting ready to leave, I put one arm in my coat and tried to zip it up that way. Susan was laughing hysterically. "We should photograph you like that," she said. Outside the weather was bitter, bitter cold. So cold that while we put things in the car, my fingers were frozen red. (Barb)

❀

The winds continued on our drive to Raleigh, NC, and the cold pursued us. But all the piney forest along the road was green. A roadside sign said, "Believe You Can," to my amazement.
Through Haw River.
The Sam Hunt Freeway.
Exit 219.
(MO)

❀

I remember the land starting to slope and the freeways beginning to curve. The low scrubby winter trees and grass started turning into taller brown trees, and finally into pine trees. Once as we were driving through the pines, I looked ahead up a hill, the sun overhead (we were going south), and all the cars coming our way were gleaming.

While driving, we talked a lot about our past relationships, happy to presently be living alone. We told stories about the people we had met at the reading, food, politics. We had a long conversation about the books we read when we were young. I read a lot of Louisa May Alcott, Laura Ingalls Wilder, Mark Twain, and Charles Dickens and all the books on the shelves in the school library. What Maureen loved reading when she was very young was Albert Payson Terhune's stories about collies; later she liked reading Carson McCullers, Dostoevsky, Louisa May Alcott, Eudora Welty's short stories, and so many others. Both of our mothers took us frequently to the public libraries. We both remember the excitement of coming home carrying big stacks of books to read.

On the 22nd, we woke up in Raleigh, NC, in a Doubletree Hilton, a special deal, these first three hotels on Maureen's AAA membership. We did our yoga practices (I'm teaching Maureen). Then we piled our many bags into our car and started driving another three-hundred-mile stretch. As we drove along, I asked Maureen how she got involved in writing poetry. She said when she was young, she was up in the family attic and found an Irish songbook with rhyming verses. She remembers becoming excited and later at eight or nine writing an epic poem about the life of a blue butterfly. I remember lying on the ground and staring at the leaves in the trees; I wrote a haiku for my high school English teacher. That was my start.

After a mistaken turnoff, we took I-85 Business for a while. I remember passing by a Giant Peach with the name Gaffney on it. "I think they grow peaches here," I said. Later I googled and discovered that Gaffney is in Cherokee County, South Carolina, and is known as "The Peach Capital of South Carolina." But only .45% Native Americans live there. (Barb)

❋

Up early in Raleigh for yoga and buckwheat breakfast, then on our way to South Carolina. The geography begins to roll into curving hills and the road waves up and down.

The pines stay green and the weather begins to thaw. Tonight, we cook our dinner in the tradition of traveling Hindu women in the bathroom of our hotel room. Barbara has brought all the spices and tiny pots along. (MO)

Onward to Pensacola, FL

January, 23 - 26, 2019

Here we are in Pensacola sitting across from each other in the dining room. We are both trying to recapture and rethink our past three days on the road. We open an email from Terence Winch, with a link to his blog **"The Best American Poetry"** about our road trip and with a transcript of the reading we did in his impressive basement/studio before we left his house. (MO/Barb)

❈

We read Terence's post and laughed at his description of our car full of things. Then I told Maureen a story about Iris Adler, an artist I met in the early '90s at Byrdcliffe Arts Colony. She had an old van full of what looked like junk but was in fact valuable items for making her sculptures. She was much older than me and was traveling from one colony to another. Once she told me a story about how she managed to be an artist and a mother at the same time. She said something like this (as I remember), "When my children were young, I wasn't much of a cook. For their school lunches I would make enough peanut butter sandwiches for a week and freeze them." Iris and I laughed and now Maureen and I were laughing. We understood because we had also raised children. (Barb)

❈

We left Anderson, SC, on January 23rd, heading to Atlanta, GA, on I-85 South. Peaceful driving along and over the North Fork Broad River and on. Cloudy sky with rain pending, but the landscape became more and more beautiful. In Montgomery we found our hotel in a cluster of others on the outskirts. We cooked in, as we had splurged in Anderson and gone to P.F. Chang's. The Best Western we stayed at had the most obliging cooking situation of any of the hotels so far. Outside there was a cloudburst of rain that Barbara got caught in as she ran out to the local organic store for a couple of things needed for our dinner. We had buckwheat noodles and veggies and went overboard with some Havarti cheese. After our repast we caught up on the daily news. Go Nancy Pelosi! (MO)

❃

We stopped in LaGrange, Georgia, looking for a lunch spot, came upon Gus's Grill, but first we decided to walk around the plaza with a statue of Lafayette and a fountain. After that, we were too late. Gus's had closed. Back on the road.

As we drove further south, little by little we took off layers of coats and undercoats. Still cold and somewhat damp, but curvy, and the landscape more beautiful even when overcast. As we were ending our drive in Georgia, the last thirty miles, we traveled on a back road so we could see the world behind the manicured freeway. Maureen took the wheel, still a little leery because she had not driven a stick in many years, but very quickly she remembered. (Barb)

(Barb)

All the hotel rooms were okay, but the air was stuffy. Upon arrival, we turned on MSNBC and caught up with the antics of our destructive president. We clapped when Pelosi said, "No, sorry, you can't give a speech in the House until the shutdown is over." Then we rolled with laughter when the bully tweeted something like: "I *decided* not to give the speech until after the shutdown."

Every morning we religiously did our yoga practices. I am teaching Maureen and every day she is becoming more and more limber. (Barb)

❈

Early morning on the 24th, we left Montgomery on a highway flat grey as the sky above, but no rain today. It's cooler tho because of the downpour last night. Suddenly green grass! Gas is $1.89. Large birds soared overhead. Turkey vultures or hawks? The ditches along the road were mowed here and formed lovely clean, green mounds. Lots of pastureland and cattle. We chatted about Southern writers and how the South is so literary. They love poetry and stories and seem more romantic. We wondered if the warmer, easier weather promotes a more easy-going lifestyle. And then the sun came out! (MO)

❈

On the 24th, our GPS directed us off the main highway (84 to 65) and on to a few smaller highways. As we drove along, the air started feeling different, more like the ocean, the houses, similar to the houses I remember in New Orleans, spread out with big porches. The accents of the people in the gas stations became thicker with a Southern slant. Jamey Jones and Rachael Pongetti were still teaching so we went straight to a funky warm vegan restaurant I liked when I was here in Pensacola a few years earlier, End of the Line Café. Maureen and I sat at a table by the window looking out at the train tracks across the way. (Barb)

(MO)

It was too early to go to the house of our hosts, Jamey Jones and Rachael Pongetti, and we wanted to see the water as we were so close. We didn't know exactly how to get to it, so I picked another restaurant, Cactus Cantina, that was on North 12th Avenue and looked to be right on the Gulf. We set our GPS for the cantina, but it drove us around in circles, finally we got to the cantina, but the airport was between us and the water! We couldn't see it at all! We gave up and drove to Jamey and Rachael's. Already the signs of warmer climes. Huge oaks and magnolia trees. Camellia bushes. Their place is right on the Bayou. (MO)

As we sat in front of Jamey and Rachael's house waiting for them, we watched some workmen packing up their things (their house is being renovated). Ten minutes later Jamey and Rachael arrived and welcomed us into their abode, where they live with Luna, an energetic little spotted dog, and Jeff the fish. (Barb/MO)

(MO/Barb)

After unloading all our things into a mound in Jamey and Rachael's front room, they gave us a tour of their fabulous house where Jamey had grown up with his siblings. Built about 1924, Jamey's dad had later rather "1950'd" the house up, probably to make it different than it was while he was growing up. Now Jamey and Rachael are restoring some of the original glory as they also update and modernize. Gorgeous patinas on some of the molding and the stairway to the spacious attic, that Jamey had spent months emptying of family treasures. A big, new window illuminated the space and light bounced off the wooden floor. Now, just moving in while workers continue to finish the outside and roof, they too had boxes and possessions piled about. Where things were in the big, bright, new kitchen was anyone's guess. The magnificent tall windows were key throughout the house. Rushing up the walls, they flooded the rooms with light. Even in its unfinished state, Jamey's boyhood home glowed. (MO)

❀

When we arrived, I was happy to be back in Pensacola with my friends, Rachael and Jamey. **Jamey Jones** is a poet who came to the MFA program at LIU as an already established poet. Then we became friends while working together on his thesis. He and Rachael had moved back into this house shortly before we arrived. The house was beautifully renovated, a house that Jamey grew up in. His grandfather lived there too. As we walked around the house, Jamey said, "This is my grandfather's footprint . . . The eaves were still there when my grandfather was here, then my father added plywood . . . See this hook? Two of them fell out when the carpenters were working. My grandmother used these exact hooks to weave in the room where you are staying. She had one in each corner . . ." I looked at the screw. An ordinary tiny metal hook with carving at the base. I said to Jamey, "Why don't you make a list poem of all the connections to past generations?" While we swept, moved boxes into the corner, and filled up a gigantic airbed where I would sleep, Maureen and Rachel went on a walk with Luna dog, down a few blocks to see the Bayou. (Barb)

❉

Luna pulled us along like a little speckled spirit. The Bayou was water! And so pretty in the setting sun. Then I saw my first albino squirrel! As it leaped like a small ghost through the snarly branches of an ancient oak, I felt for a second like I was in the Japanese horror movie *Kuroneko*.

Trees abound: magnolia, live and water oak, crepe myrtle, sweetgum, juniper, cedar, pecan, pine, and palm. Camellia bushes across the drive.

That evening we four went to the End of the Line again for a three-course vegan meal. (MO)

(MO)

Back at their place we sat up late into the night over wine and books. Jamey and I found we had both been wildly inspired early on in our writing by Gregory Corso's *The Happy Birthday of Death* and *Gasoline*. We marveled at the mystery of how we all seemed to randomly find, in so unpredictable a way, the writers and the path that brought us to our work. As tho some mysterious part of our being was looking for it, and then rather stumbled upon these connections. (MO)

(Barb)

While I was sitting in the rocker with eye patches warming my dry eyes, I listened to Jamey and Maureen talking. Blindly, I piped up, "You two really have found each other." Lots of fun always at the dining room table. Jamey and Rachael are both exuberant and excited about art, poetry, and love of others. (Barb)

❋

Rachael talked about her photography and showed me some pieces. I immediately fell in love with the edginess of her work. She spoke about her teaching methods and I so wanted to take her classes. I pulled out my iPhone and showed her a series of photos I took of the pine forests on a train trip through the High Sierras when it was snowing heavily. She said I had an "eye," which filled me with joy as I love photography. (MO)

❋

For the first time in a week, Maureen and I were able to sleep in separate rooms. Blissful to be away from the bags of kitchen things and alone.

On Friday the 21st, I woke up to hear men banging around the house outside. We washed our clothes and rearranged things, starting to find some kind of order for our travels on the road. When Rachael and Jamey left for school, Maureen and I did our yoga practices. While we were doing yoga, the men were working on the eaves outside our window and we pretended not to see them, and they pretended not to see us. While I was packing up, one man caught my eye and I waved to him. When we went out to the car to find a restaurant for lunch, I stopped to talk to them. "Did you enjoy practicing yoga with us?" I asked. They laughed. "Even watching can transmit energy." (Barb)

❀

We spent the morning catching up on this blog. Then we went to lunch at the Five Sisters Blues Café, an amazing blues venue with posters yellowed and new covering the walls. (MO)

❀

Back at the house I took Loony Tune for a walk around the block. Something about this dog—I really like her. Energetic, sleek, and on her own journey, dashing around, but then she comes back for a petting session. Then Jamey came home, and Luna wanted to go out again. The cats wanted to come in. Maureen's stomach was churning. She fell asleep on the sofa. Rachael came in the door and fell asleep in her bedroom. (Barb)

❀

Rachael arrived with lots of yummy food. But I had to decline dinner and sit in their chocolate brown recliner with a bit of a stomach upset. Too much wine, no doubt, and too much new and varied diet of the trip. Rachael brought me tea and Jamey's grandmother's soft fog-colored blanket. She was feeding Jeff the fish and told me the story. She said she hadn't intended to get a fish, but some students had brought in goldfish for an assignment and one of them mentioned his fish was up for adoption. Rachael had had a good friend who died in high school and his name was Jeff. When she asked the fish's name, the student said Jeff. "Did you name him after someone you know?" she asked. And he said he didn't know anyone named Jeff. (MO)

Jan. 26, 2019. Jamey and I take Luna for her morning walk around a few blocks and along the Bayou. Birds are singing like spring. The bayou shimmers blue in the crispy sun. Jamey has cousins and relatives aplenty here. As we walk, three boys go by on their bikes. We exchange hellos and Jamey says, "That's my cousin." Growing up on the racetrack and moving from place to place, I marvel at what a sense of rootedness this must bring.

Jamey, Rachel, and I went to Pensacola Beach. We headed out under the famous trestle bridge known as Graffiti Bridge that **Rachael Pongetti** took photos of daily for a year, recording the ever-changing graffiti art that folks add to and paint over constantly, creating a phenomenal book. Across Pensacola Bay, the Gulf of Mexico was just a skip and a jump away. As I walked up over the dunes to the water, I was struck by a view of the sea I'd never experienced before. Because of the way the dune dipped the sea appeared to stand up as tho a huge wave was suspended in air or held against glass. But the tide washed in lightly over a thigh-deep trough where a man was gathering shells. The sea was the color of illuminated aquamarine. The sand was pure white and soft as silk. It was an optical illusion of sorts that was overwhelmingly beautiful and at the same time it felt mysteriously dangerous as the water stood up so high above us. Neither Jamey or Rachael seemed to see anything odd about the view and I wondered if I'd entered some kind of altered reality after days of driving. It's a scene I'll never forget.

We said hello to the man gathering shells. He asked our names and said his name was Broken. He explained that he gathered the shells in the trough as they were not crushed apart as the ones on the beach were. He showed us what he had so far, and his shells were totally whole and perfect unlike the scattered chipped ones on the beach. Not broken, I thought, reflecting on his name. As we parted Jamey said casually how good it was to meet him. Suddenly wary, he asked, "What did you say?" Jamey repeated and Broken thanked him. "I really appreciate that," he said. (MO)

Photo by Rachael Pongetti

I stayed home to spend time preparing for the reading. I had rarely read from *Just Like That* to an audience and I wanted to prepare a ten-minute dip into the story that would work while also reading poems. The novel is about a relationship that starts and stops, starts and stops, and so forth and so on. Instead of reading a section dwelling on the emotions of the halting, I found another section where the narrator is writing a poem very close to a poem I once wrote :-). Then I fell asleep for an hour and woke up as the group came back into the house. Maureen gave me a clam shell she had found on the beach and that I tucked away in a safe place in my suitcase. I regretted missing the beach, but our bodies also require sleep and care.

A few hours later, after much chatting, we went to the Pensacola Museum of Art for our reading. Grade school kids' art covered the walls. There was a big crowd, many of Jamey's students and other artists and poets from the community were there. I recognized several who were at my last reading (and workshop) in town a few years earlier. When Maureen was reading her poems from *Erosion's Pull*, I recognized some of the lines (especially from "Whenever I snow . . ."). In 2007, ***Talisman*** published an interview I had conducted with Maureen about her process and background for the poems in this collection. (Barb)

(Barb)

Photo by Rachael Pongetti

After the reading, Rachael rushed home to finish cooking delicious vegetarian lasagna and a crowd of friends came to the house for a party. At 1 a.m. we crawled into our beds and so did Luna, Jeff, and the kitties, Oscarella, Macey, and Finn. (MO)

Photo of Barb signing book with Pat Rowe. In back, Jamey speaking with Chris Pappas.
In front. Racheal, Rick Voeltz and Richard McCabe. *(MO)*
Photo of Maureen talking with Pat. In back, Rachael with Rick. *(Barb)*

ONWARD TO MOBILE

JANUARY, 27 - 28, 2019

After we left Jamie and Rachael's house, we stopped at the Leisure Club Coffee Bar in Pensacola to continue working on our blog. At eleven we hit the road to Mobile, Alabama. An hour later we arrived at the Botanical Gardens. We were an hour early, hoping to find a café, but no café. A man outside the gate, Lynn, kindly escorted us to the garden's learning center where we were to read. He unlocked the door and we found a pleasant carpeted room set up with refreshments in back. In front, there was a wicker chair beside an end table with a light and a microphone, and standing in the corner, a mock-gardener, scarecrow-like figure with an actual deer's head mounted on top. (Barb)

❀

At the Mobile Botanical Gardens, storks and egrets were wading around in the garden's ponds. The day was overcast, but not too cold. What a delightful garden! We headed toward a stately building behind an ornate wrought iron gate near the parking lot. The keeper of the gate's name was Lynn, a charming, sprite-like gentleman with a wry sense of humor. He walked us up to the well-set up room where the reading would take place. (MO)

❀

We set up our books in back and waited for **Sue B. Walker** to arrive. Sue is the publisher of Negative Capability Press and past poet laureate of Alabama; I have known her for a number of years, first as a student in my writers.com classes (more like a co-teacher) and then as a friend. I was happy to be able to respond to some of the poems she later included in her latest really phenomenal collection poems about the women writers in her life, *Let Us Imagine Her Name*. Later she published my book, *A Day Like Today,* and I read a few years earlier at a salon at her house. (Barb)

❊

Our host Sue Walker arrived as we were setting out our pamphlet and books. A wonderful, energetic writer, editor, and organizer of readings and events. Definitely check out her book *Let Us Imagine Her Name* from Clemson University Press. (MO)

Photo by Jami Buck

Sue asked me to introduce Maureen. I wasn't prepared and Maureen whispered, "Just read the bio in the back of our book." I did that and also talked about how she had grown up on a farm and if they listened closely, they might hear the sounds of Minnesota farmland in her poems. (Barb)

Left: *Photo by Barb*. Right: *Photo by Jami Buck*

After we both read, we took some questions from an audience composed mostly of writers, professors, and artists. Barbara and I responded to pertinent questions on our writing process and on whether poetry played a more visible part in our culture in past decades as opposed to contemporary times. We discussed rhyme and the importance of rhythm in the poetic line. Then a delightful reception with much chatting and connecting. (MO)

(MO)

After the reading and questions, a quiet spoken woman approached me to sign some books, Marilyn Johnston. She told me that she was also from Detroit. "Where exactly?" I asked. "East Detroit," she said. I was shocked. We were both from the same four-square mile city, a suburb of Detroit, now called East Pointe. As I have traveled around the country, I've never met anyone who came from there. Then she told me that she had attended East Detroit High School, the same school I attended, but had graduated ten years earlier than me in 1956. And she also had worked for Chrysler Motor Company until she retired, like my father, she in market research for new cars, my father, first on the line and then as a draftsman working on government contracts. That's the story of Detroit. Almost everyone has relatives in the car companies. Marilyn now lives in Mobile, close to her son. (Barb)

❀

We followed our host for the evening, **Lindsey Hannahan**, poet and painter, to her home where we met Bella the Bassett. We were introduced to her youngest daughter, Grace. At dinner and drinks we thoroughly enjoyed getting to know Lindsey. She has a book of poems soon to come out from Negative Capability Press. The next morning at breakfast she showed me some of her paintings and we talked about some of the poems in her forthcoming book. (MO)

A selfie with Lindsey

Lindsey's house was a sprawling Southern-style home. Once I went the wrong way looking for Maureen's room and I almost couldn't find my way back. Then we holed up in my room in an extremely comfortable bed for an hour or two working on our Pensacola blog post. (Barb)

Poetry Readings
at the Mobile Botanical Gardens
Sunday, January 27th

Maureen Owen's most recent book is *Edges of Water*, Chax Press. Other books include: *Erosion's Pull*, Coffee House Press, finalist for the Colorado Book Award; *American Rush: Selected Poems*, finalist for the L.A. Times Book Prize; and *AE (Amelia Earhart)*, Before Columbus American Book Award. She was the publisher and editor of *Telephone Magazine/Telephone Books*. Maureen lives in Denver and has taught for Naropa University. Her readings can be found on PennSound.

Barbara Henning is the author of four novels and seven collections of poetry. Most recent books are a novel, *Just Like That* (Spuyten Duyvil) and a book of poetry, *A Day Like Today* (Negative Capability Press). She is also the editor of a book of interviews, *Looking Up Harryette Mullen*, and *The Collected Prose of Bobbie Louise Hawkins*. Barbara lives in Brooklyn, has taught for Naropa University and Long Island University where she is Professor Emerita. Her website is *barbarahenning.com*

What: Join us for poetry readings from two accomplished authors! Light refreshments will be provided.

Selected readings from:
Maureen Owen – *Edges of Water* (Chax Press), *Erosion's Pull* (Coffee House Press), and *Imaginary Income* (Hanging Loose Press)
Barbara Henning – *Just Like That* (Spuyten Duyvil) and *A Day Like Today* (Negative Capability Press)

Where: Mobile Botanical Gardens *(4 min drive from University of South Alabama)*
   5151 Museum Drive
   Mobile, AL 36608

When: Sunday, January 27th from 2pm - 4pm

Admission: NonMem- General Admission - $5
      Members - Free
      Donations always welcome!

NEW ORLEANS

JANUARY 28 - 30, 2019

Jan. 28, 2019. On the road to New Orleans, as I was driving, I asked Maureen to look up **David and Roselyn**, a musician couple that I knew from Detroit back in the late '70s. For a while they lived and travelled in a bus with their children and a few other people. In earlier years, I had spent a lot of time in New Orleans (a boyfriend had family there); now and again I would run into David and Roselyn performing in the French Quarter. I was wondering if they were still there and hoping we would see them. While I was driving, Maureen read the following description:

David [Leonard] and Roselyn [Lionheart] met while touring Air Force bases in 1959. They took a detour from music for David to get an anthropology degree from Berkeley while Roselyn became president of Berkeley Congress of Racial Equality and president of the Berkeley/Oakland Democratic Party. Their first trip to New Orleans together came while they were registering voters in Louisiana in 1963 and learning to play the blues in juke joints around the state. They played by their campfires throughout the west and folks would gather around them and invite them to join them at their campsites and suggested they should be professional musicians. Their first gig was in the Cass Corridor in Detroit where they were billed as David & Zelda. They have played around the world and they are going again.

Below is an early photo of David and Roselyn, posted by Dennis Pruss, a Detroiter, on Tribes of the Cass Corridor website. (Barb)

DAVID & ROSELYN

Photo by Dennis Pruss

In NOLA, we walked eight blocks along Royal Street looking for a particular restaurant, and then we discovered that we were going in the wrong direction. Fortunately, our wrong turn stopped us in our tracks, mesmerized by an African American woman singing a blues song. She turned and looked into my eyes while she was singing and I felt teary. She had such a beautiful voice and spirit. As we went along, I asked a few musicians if they knew David and Roselyn. Finally, one said yes, they are usually down on Royal and Louisiana. But he added that he had not seen them in a while. The last post we found online was from 2016. I remember them singing "The Beaubien Street Blues" in Detroit clubs. (Barb)

❀

When we arrived in New Orleans, we found our lovely little Airbnb, courtesy of Bill Lavender. Unloaded the car and took a twenty-block walk to the French Quarter. It was so elating to be in New Orleans!

So warm and sunny and full of colors. We ate dinner at Bennachin, a delicious African restaurant. Then, exhausted from walking around, we hailed a cab that drove us in and out of streets, turning this way and that, unnecessarily taking us on a much longer route home than we had walked. But only charging us the fare we had been promised. Curious, and a little scary. (MO)

(MO)

Kind of late on the 28th, Maureen and I sat in the small living room in the back of our New Orleans apartment on St. Philip Street in Mid-City New Orleans. We had spent most of our free time writing our blog. When we were bleary eyed, one of us said, "Let's watch something on TV." What a good decision to watch *Roma*, our first movie of the trip, a black and white Netflix film. What is it about black and white? It jars your sense of reality and makes you more aware of the art of the film. Also, it harkens back in time. And this film (by director and writer Alfonso Cuarón) is set in the 1970s when many of us were still watching black and white television.

The film starts out very slowly focusing on the daily activities of a comfortably middle-class family in Mexico City, mother, father, four children, and two maids. The beginning of the film was focused on daily activities; I was reminded of Klaus Knausgaard's novels; unlike

Knausgaard, here the camera follows someone other than the narrator, in this case, a housemaid, Clio, who is very loving, tender, and naively involved with a lousy guy who is being trained by the government to be a soldier. Simultaneously the mother, Sofia, is dealing with a husband-professor who abandons her and the children. Little by little, slowly and quietly, the problems accrue for Clio until finally she finds herself in the middle of a horrifying attack on student demonstrators, her boyfriend one of the attackers. I loved the slowness of this film, the black and white shots that zoomed in on ordinary, unbeautiful objects, like a pile of dog poop. I also appreciated the way female nudity was not used to titillate. Instead, a completely naked man does martial art moves, showing off for Clio. I also loved the way at first, we begin to recognize her difficult life as a maid, but then it becomes clear that she is part of the family and when she is undergoing extreme difficulties, Sofia does not abandon her; the two women bond. When the movie was over, it was already 1 a.m. and we crawled into our beds, me into my lovely sleeping bag inside the covers, always somewhat cold inside, in the Southern climate, when the temperature drops down to thirty degrees. (Barb)

❋

After yoga and breakfast on the 29th, we walked a few blocks up Rendon Street to Esplanade in a sunny but sharp, cold wind. It seems the cold just can't stop following us. Coffee shops and cafés greeted us. We accelerated our pace to Café Degas which looked so warm and inviting, tucked away in a thicket of bushes and trees between streets. Then we heard two women wailing, "It's closed on Tuesdays!" Yes, it was Tuesday. Bracing into a bitter wind we made fast tracks for Fair Grinds Coffeehouse, the first other place in sight. They had no decaf coffee at all to my disappointment, but we stayed and worked on our blog, with the idea we'd go to another café in a bit that had decaf lattes. So after working for a while, we walked a couple of doors over to 1000 Figs and were so enticed with their menu and atmosphere that we had lunch. I never did get coffee.

We picked up a few things at the big market on the corner and found walking back not as cold. Things were squeaky clean from a big rainstorm during the night and the sun made it all shine.

We added photos to our blog. Barbara spoke to an old friend of hers and made plans to see her tonight. Bill Lavender, a poet, editor, and teacher living in New Orleans, and his wife Nancy emailed inviting us to a reading by a good friend of theirs, a New Orleanian, **Maurice Carlos Ruffin**, debuting his new novel, *We Cast a Shadow*. Bill founded *Lavender Ink*, a small press devoted mainly to poetry in 1995, and he more recently has founded *Diálogos*, an imprint devoted to cross-cultural literature. (MO)

❀

I drove over to my friend Marie Scavetta's house. We had been friends when our children were growing up. Her son, Amando, and my son, Michah, were best friends since the time they were about seven years old. When Marie opened the door to the duplex, I was surprised to learn that Armando was living in NOLA too, working as a high school teacher. He was living in one side of the duplex with his wife, Frida, and their two little girls. I took a photo, a bundle of love. I always admired Marie because, as a lawyer, she had dedicated her practice to helping people receive legal aid in NYC and here in New Orleans. For years she represented prisoners on death row. While we caught up, we ate bowls of mustard greens with garlic, cheese, and naan bread. When Armando came home from teaching high school, he explained to his oldest daughter—"When I was just a little older than you, I was over at Barbara's apartment all the time." And I said, "Yes, you and Michah were going back and forth, from our house to yours, trying to find a place where no adults were at home, so you could do whatever, whenever." (Barb)

(Barb)

As we walked the couple of blocks to the event, Nancy and Bill re-
marked how all the shops were so new that they hadn't even seen them
before. What used to be a print shop, a Dixie Stove shop, The Dollar
Bill Bar, were now chichi mod clothing stores, and tight, upscale,
sparse-looking fronts.

The Ace Hotel in the business district hosted the book reading and
signing. A high-ceilinged, new hotel that retroed old New Orleans with
its dark wood interior, tall ceilings, and romantic lighting; it hosted
the event in a wide, cozy room with an upstairs balcony. We got drinks
from one of the two bars and went upstairs with the overflow crowd.
Nancy had gone to congratulate Maurice and had him sign her book
downstairs. A fellow writer and close friend, who had gotten together
with Maurice regularly when they both were working on their separate
novels, gave a lively, thoughtful, punctuated-with-jokes-about-them
introduction. Maurice, who seemed loved by everyone in the packed
crowd, then read an excerpt from his novel. I wanted to buy a copy, but
restrained myself as too many books in our car. Made a note to do so
when I got home. Then his editor at Random House, a bright snappy
New Yorker, fielded questions to him about the novel. It made me want
to buy a copy all the more.

Nancy had made dinner reservations for us in the hotel restaurant and we tiptoed downstairs as the Q&A was wrapping. A friend of theirs, Darlene Wolnik, joined us. Darlene is a sustainable food worker and coordinates with farmers markets, giving lectures all over the US for NOLA and Cleveland, and applying for grants, etc. She started the farmers market in NOLA. Dinner was delicious and we decided to share a Black Forest dessert. When the dessert arrived, we thought it was a mistake and hailed the waitress that it was not what we had ordered. It in no way resembled what we expected. Instead, a mound of raspberry-like sauce, a mound of greyish lump, a big swirl of crumbled nuts dabbed with one tiny squirt of chocolate, and two curls of bitter chocolate thin as transparent seashells. Our waiter, looking a bit apologetic, explained that the chef created deconstructionist cuisine and this was a deconstructed Black Forest cake. "Er, well, okay," we said. We dug in and it was quite tasty, and would have been tastier, no doubt, if we had not expected a rich chocolate cakey delight. Eating it we realized we should have gotten a heads up from the rest of the meal, which tho absolutely delicious, had little outward appearance of what we envisioned we ordered. (MO)

Nancy and Bill Lavender *(MO)*

Early afternoon on the 30th, we went to PJ's Coffee, a place where Barbara had frequented in earlier years. We worked there, preparing our reading and working on our last blog post. A young woman at a table across from us was happy to snap our photo.

That night, we read at the Dragonfly Poetry and Performance Ritual Space. The reading was organized and hosted by **Megan Burns.** The crowd was smaller than our other events, but the audience was into poetry, attentive and interactive. *(Barb/MO)*

Megan Burns *(MO)*

Bill Lavender, Barbara, Maureen, Megan, and Rodger Kamenetz

In the morning as we were leaving, we found a bag of books hanging on our door from both of Bill's poetry presses, **Lavender Ink** and **Diálogos**. Be sure to check out the website. On our way to Austin (via a night in Beaumont), we stopped for gas at Breaux Bridge, LA, and Maureen snapped this snappy store. *(Barb/MO)*

(MO)

Austin & Beyond
January 31 - February 4, 2019

Jan. 31, 2019. As we headed out of NOLA, a man pulled up alongside us at a stoplight and motioned. We rolled down the window and he said, "I know two good looking white women like you wouldn't be worrying about getting any trouble 'bout it, but your brake light is out on the right side. If it was me, I'd be worrying, cause they'd be coming after me!" He was a sweet, funny fellow, laughing as he talked.

We drove long stretches of LA. St. Charles came up on I-10 West as we listened to Ray Charles sing, "Tell your mama, tell your pa, I'm gonna send you back to Arkansas." News flash: Every Senate Republican backs a rebuke of Trump's troop withdrawal from Syria and Afghanistan. We didn't brake when we saw a police car and resolved to replace the light when we got to Beaumont.

    In Texas 3:01

    Speed limit 75 (MO)

❀

Feb. 1, 2019. In the morning in Beaumont, Texas, we set up our mats in between the beds and did our yoga practices, then downstairs we ate some grits in the "complimentary breakfast." After loading the car, we stopped at a gas station to ask where we could get a brake light. We were directed around the corner to a truck repair. The young man kindly took apart the inside entry for the light and showed me how to install it. He then sent us to an auto supply. We left Beaumont without worrying any longer about the police stopping us and confiscating my old Honda with all our kitchenware and books. (Barb)

❋

Foggy then thin sun. Over Trinity River, then overcast & fog again. Darker skies. We chat about our past and places we've lived. A host of trucks on the highway and now pastures of Texas longhorns. (MO)

❋

I don't remember much about the four hours of driving along I-10 to 71. Pretty flat, one big frightening power plant, then a little strip of curvy roads and we came into Austin. (Barb)

❋

When we arrived in Austin we drove to the University of Texas, where our hosts for the night taught. The campus was vast and we drove, confused about where we were supposed to meet **John Hartigan,** Barbara's friend. We called him on the cell and after driving in what seemed familiar circles, we finally saw him gesturing to us. We had some time before Rebecca, our other host, would be ready, so Johnny gave us a tour of part of the enormous campus. Fifty thousand students go to UT. We strolled uphill to the famous turtle pond and took some quick pics of the many basking turtles. Then walked by an amazing sculpture of stainless steel and aluminum replicas of canoes intertwined by Nancy Rubins, titled "Monochrome for Austin." I snapped photos from all its jutting angles. (MO)

(MO)

In Austin we stayed at Johnny Hartigan and Rebecca Lyle's house for two nights. I've known Johnny since he was about nine years old. He is family to me. His mother was (and still is) a dear friend and when Johnny was a child, he traveled to carnivals and fairs with my husband, Allen; they had a special bond with each other.

Rebecca and Johnny kindly offered us shelter, food, laundry, and great conversation. We stayed with them for two nights. They are music lovers—Johnny plays the accordion, dobro, and concertina, and Becca plays the mandolin. See below for a wall in their living room. Johnny is an anthropologist; in his last book, *Care of the Species*, he examines botanical gardens, writing an ethnography of plants, race, and biodiversity. He is now working on an ethnography of wild horses in Galicia, Spain. Rebecca also works for UT, educating and managing a large group of high school teachers, who then teach their students college level statistics. (Barb)

(Barb)

That night, we had dinner together with Johnny and Rebecca's daughter, Zia, and her friend at a vegan restaurant called The Beer Plant, thereby making all of us happy, those who drink beer and those who don't (me). When Zia arrived, I was surprised at how much she still looked like the little girl who spent the night with me in 2005 in Tesuque, New Mexico; now she's a beautiful, vibrant young woman studying civil engineering. It wasn't long ago when women did not major in Engineering. Hurray for Zia. The next day we had lunch at Sour Duck Market, another crazy, beautiful, delicious place. And the next night at Spider House Café. (Barb)

Feb. 2, 2019. In the morning the weather was still misty and damp. Austin is close enough to the gulf to share the humidity with desert plant life. I went on a hike with Johnny, heading down a path behind his house through a wooded area, following a dry creek to a flood plain and finally ending at the public library (possibly three miles). (Barb)

(Barb)

Thanks to Becky Garcia at Malvern Books. She did a great job of organizing their space for our reading and also announcing and promoting the reading. Fernando set up a table with our books and Rebekah introduced the three of us. There was a big attentive crowd. We read with **Ashley Smith-Keyfitz**, a young, exciting Austin poet. (Barb/MO)

❊

Michael Anania, longtime friend, poet, essayist, and fiction writer, who I hadn't seen since I had reddish hair and he had black, came to our reading at Malvern Books. Fabulous to see him again after so long a time! We had fun catching up a bit and in his usual energetic fashion he turned me onto one of the books on display: *Duets* by Edward Byrne, a little book that tests the boundaries of translation. I'll say no more, but you must check it out as Michael's excitement about it is not to be questioned. (MO)

(Barb)

Photos by Malvern Staff

Three Poets' Shoes

Photo by Malvern Staff

Malvern Books sent us a link to a cool photo and links to **Barbara, Maureen,** and **Ashley**'s readings. After the reading, we went out with Ashley Smith-Keyfitz and Ben Keyfitz. We ordered vegan sandwiches from a food truck parked outside Spider House; apparently there are hundreds of food trucks in Austin. We sat outside in the misty weather eating our burgers and chatting about poetry, Austin, New York, families and . . . (Barb/MO)

Ashley & Ben *(MO)*

(MO)

Feb. 3, 2019. On the road to our motel in Sweetwater, Texas, as we passed by miles of grazing and farmland, one of our more interesting conversations was about Maureen's potato farm. She owns some property in Minnesota, the farm where she grew up. The house is ramshackle now, maybe collapsed, but she has this idea that she will put up some temporary structure, like a little trailer or a yurt or something like that and she'll go out there for a few months of the year and raise potatoes to donate mostly to an organization that supports the homeless, and maybe selling just enough to pay her electricity for the year. It will be called "The Bud Phalen Potato Project," after her uncle who farmed that land. I see her there on a flat country landscape digging and planting potatoes and at night lying on the hood of her car, looking up at the stars, and writing poetry. (Barb)

❀

As we neared Sweetwater, TX, the landscape became an enormous wind farm. Literally hundreds of wind turbines, their elegant slender bodies, creamy white and stunning, engulfed the hilly view. They seemed to go on forever and we noted that tho the development of wind power is a boon to the environment, the problem of their wreaking havoc on migrating birds and waterfowl is a grave one. We chatted on noting that this was an issue that was being investigated. I thought I'd read somewhere that some kind of sonar device was being worked on that could be installed in the turbines and would signal our feathered friends to avoid that area. But we agreed it was still a complicated issue. Improving the environment yet wounding the creatures in the environment. (MO)

❀

One Eye Open & Driving

One eye open, the other still sleeping
yoga between beds, reach up, wake up
curtains drawn, passersby pass by
sky blue and wide, Texas style
pumping gas, a cow braying in a trailer
miles and miles of wind mills
a dry treeless main street town
Post Texas library with no bathrooms
love of the word, pee in McDonalds
no such thing as decaf, a donut
from Donut Depot for Maureen,
all of a sudden Lubbock &
a scruffy guy with a cigarette
dangling lays down his bike

and snaps us beside Buddy Holly's
glasses, sun in my eyes, hello
from Cricket Street to Broadway,
urban coffee decaf and Turmeric Latte,
then off we go tracing the wires,
along US 84W, listening to Arthur Blythe
remembering entering Alvin's Finer
under Blythe sound with Allen
& with Detroit friends, flat flat
land in 4 directions, finally hot,
in the *Times* read out loud
about prisoners in Brooklyn,
without heat, zero degrees, banging
on the walls & we're 26 miles to Clovis
and Mexican food at Leal's,
just a hop skip & jump to our beds
(Barb)

(Barb)

Feb. 4, 2019. *For Patrick   Happy Birthday*

Left the very fine Microtel Inn in Sweetwater, TX, headed for Clovis, NM. Driving straight along beside acres and acres of graceful and elegant wind turbines, we looked for a town with a coffee shop. In Slaton we found Donut Depot, but no coffee or tea after 11:30 a.m. And definitely no decaf. I'm finding Texas does not do decaf. No decaf lattes. When I ask for decaf they seem to question my sanity. Like why are you drinking coffee if you don't want caffeine?

We went off route in Lubbock to see the Buddy Holly Center where a giant replica of his glasses sits out front. Being Monday, the museum was closed, but we delighted in posing beside the dark geeky frames. A man on a bicycle came by so we asked him to take our photo. He mentioned that Sunday, Feb 3rd, the day before, was a gala 60th anniversary for BH at the museum. Sigh, had we only come a day earlier, but it was great to be there now. BH was and still is my favorite rock 'n' roll singer.

In Lubbock we found a perfect coffee shop and, of course, no decaf lattes. But they did have decaf coffee, so I had steamed milk with that. Lubbock had a lot of shuttered storefronts, boarded windows, abandoned shops. Rather surprising in a city with fabulous red brick streets.

We left Lubbock for Clovis through country sides dotted with little homesteads, scrubby trees, and solitary oil rigs on little farms. (MO)

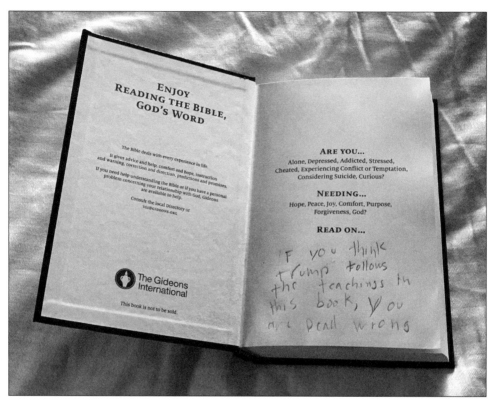

Found inside a bible in Microtel Hotel in Sweetwater, Texas

Albuquerque and Beyond
February 5 - 11, 2019

Feb. 5, 2019. Driving away from the Comfort Inn in Clovis past the Golden West Flour Co. building, we watched heavy military aircraft come in for landings. The Cannon Air Force Base is seven miles SW of Clovis. It's under the jurisdiction of Air Force Special Operations Command. The population of the base is around two thousand. More herds of pretty cattle lolled in the pastures, Angus and Hereford. The day a greyish mauve cast. Then there were rams with curving horns and sheep. Highway 84 West runs alongside the railroad track where long freight trains passed us going in the opposite direction. A dead coyote hung off a wire fence, fur ruffling in the wind, shot and left as a warning to other coyotes no doubt. What is it about New Mexico? When we crossed the border from Texas, the skies opened like a fan and unrolled all around us. Suddenly it was all sparkling blue with swirls and white puffs of clouds. A Georgia O'Keeffe painting.

Driving, we noted abandoned farmsteads and a regular old ghost town. Then Appaloosa and Buckskin in a high pasture.

Arrived in Albuquerque at the Mother Road (Route 66) Hostel. We were early and no one at the front desk, all locked up. We found a cool coffee shop nearby to wait, tho just as we sat down to enjoy our scone and tea, we saw they were closing at 3:30 and it was 3:25! They let us linger a little, then we drove back to the hostel and took a walk till they opened. The Mother Road is a bright yellow, older building with many rooms and a very accommodating atmosphere. The staff is extremely helpful and friendly and the security is top notch.

I emailed Margaret Randall, a wonderful writer and activist living in Albuquerque, and we made plans to meet for dinner tomorrow with her and her spouse, Barbara Byers, a terrific artist. (MO)

(MO)

FEB. 5 - 6, 2019

Woke up in Clovis, NM,
tired, sleeping rough
body in a vata state,
gotta calm down,
take turns, driving,
car climbing upward,
lived under this same
blue sky umbrella before,
the sloping planet earth,
eat tempeh sandwiches
& drive into Albuquerque's
mother road hostel, two
rooms pro-soundly
possible in the hostel,

dinner at Annapurna,
communal breakfast
with a guy from Ireland
en route to Mexico
another guy profoundly
in the know, political
history & all, cold and rainy,
small yoga class, slow-ga,
just what I need, the women
advise chlorophyll for
altitude sickness, coupled
with lung overuse, windy,
clear and cold, unpack
our coats, radiator cold,
missing a bullet, visit Margaret
Randall and Barbara Byers,
talking art, writing, two lives
having lived/living art, Cuba,
Roma, paintings and asemic
writing, home to Central Ave
Hwy 66, still breathless
Maureen carries my bag.
(Barb)

❀

Feb. 6, 2019. We met **Margaret Randall** and **Barbara Byers** at the Orchid Thai Cuisine on Central Avenue. We meant to take some photos with Margaret and Barbara at their house where we gathered after dinner, but we got lost in conversation and forgot. Barbara took us into her studio and showed us her art book projects, as well as some of her recent asemic work and paintings. Margaret gave us a copy of her recent collected poems. (MO)

❀

As I was sitting quietly there, a bit breathless, I noticed how beautiful Margaret was as she reclined on the couch talking to us about all her trips and adventures. I wish I had taken a snap. (Barb)

Orchid Thai Cuisine on Central Avenue *(MO)*

Feb. 7, 2019. Compared to our last reading in Austin at Malvern Books, the turnout at Bookworks in Albuquerque was a bit disappointing. The weather was unseasonably cold and apparently affected the attendance. We were very happy, however, to read for the small group that included Barbara Byers, Mark Mills (a friend of Elinor Nauen's), a few of Barb's online students, Sherry Wright and her husband David (of San Francisco), and Dara Elerath, a very talented young poet and graphic designer. Margaret Randall sent her regards; she wasn't well enough to attend. After the reading we went to the Flying Star Café with Barbara Byers and **Dara Elerath**. See Appendix C for a link to the **Reading Announcement**. (Barb/MO)

Dara Elerath, Maureen, Barbara, Barbara Byers

Saturday, Feb. 9, 2019. After dragging our stuff down the stairs and out to the front porch of the funky hostel, I went back upstairs and photographed the scene outside the window of my room. I was happy to start heading south; sloping downward, the altitude pressure let up on my lungs. Hurray for strength. (Barb)

(Barb)

Driving the 150 miles toward Truth or Consequences, my mind drifts back to driving I-25 to I-10 several times in the past, once photographing as much of the sky, rocks, mountains, mounds of dry brown dirt as I could (at the same time steering). My plan was to string it together and put it into a long foldout book, writing a poem along the top and bottom. Many of the photos are still in my archive, but the plan never came to fruition. New York City demands took over. (Barb)

❀

Adios, Albuquerque. We headed out to Truth or Consequences, NM. Peaceful, wide-open desert, then mountains came into view. We pulled into T or C and had a bite at the Passion Pie Café. Too early to check in at Rocket Inn, we strolled around and visited the Geronimo Springs Museum. A very interesting First Nations fellow, Herald, greeted us at the desk. The museum was a lot bigger than it appeared from the front. There were several rooms full of photos, well-labeled archeological native pottery, and materials from the Old West—saddles, long rifles, chaps, and frayed but charming pioneer dresses. I was especially intrigued by a chronological lifeline and photos of an Irish immigrant, who became a well-respected and upstanding member of this community, settling here some generations ago and whose sons and daughters have continued living in the area. His name was Sullivan, which is my grandmother's name and her parents immigrated to America at about the same time and from the same county in Ireland, County Cork. I found myself thinking that possibly we might be related. (MO)

❀

Waiting to check in to the Rocket Inn, after visiting the museum, we drove around Elephant Butte. The Rio Grande was almost a trickle with a big, towering dam but nothing to dam up, and a small body of water with a few houseboats in between gigantic barren rocks. The highway swerved around the upper edges of the rocks and we both agreed as we followed the curves, the whole scene was spooky. (Barb)

❀

In Truth or Consequences, we arrived at the Rocket Inn. It seemed the nicest spot so far of the motels and hotels we've stayed at. The owner, Val (who we wish now we'd taken a photo of—such a striking, cool-looking woman) had bought the inn in rundown condition about twenty-five years ago and had completely renovated it by herself. She literally did much of the physical construction updating. Our stay there was a treat. (MO)

❃

What a relief after the hostel: the Rocket Inn was clean, warm, and pleasant. And we did not have to lug our things up to the second floor. We decided that all we wanted to do was stay in the motel and rest. (Barb)

Photo by Val Wilkes

Feb. 10, 2019. Driving out the next morning across the desert to Tucson, we chatted about how lucky we were to have children despite it taking time from our writing. And how much our children mean to us. Then we mused on the marvelous flat desert with scattered bushes & low stubby grasses.

Rainstorm between Hatch & Deming. Fierce sky, but mostly wind and light rain. (MO)

❃

As we drove along the two-lane highway between Hatch and Lordsburg, to our left there was a brown storm coming, probably a sandstorm, and on all other sides dark grey clouds. I hit the gas pedal going faster. Could we beat it? Some drops fell as we cut across the desert. Whew. Not today. (Barb)

Selfie

TUCSON
FEBRUARY 11 - 17, 2019

Feb. 11, 2019. We pulled into Tucson and the first real warm weather of the tour. Barbara had lived here a few years ago and so knew her way around. We drove up N. 4th Ave, which was lined with happening restaurants, coffee shops, bookstores new and used, and lots of quirky shops. Of course, we had to go into the used bookstore first and then Antigone Books, buying a book in both! Then we went up the street to Café Passe, an old haunt of Barbara's. We hung out till our casita was available. Later we had dinner with **Charles Alexander** and his wife, Cynthia, at the New Delhi Palace. **Cynthia Miller** is a painter and art teacher. She has shown her work in NYC and other cities and is deeply involved in the art scene here in Tucson.

Drove around town. Settled in. Barbara found a Yoga studio for her practice. Emailed David and Laura Wilk, who would soon be in town for a winter stay. Will be so fun to see them as usually they are far away on the East Coast. (MO)

Cynthia Miller and
Charles Alexander
(MO)

As I drive around town showing Maureen this and that, slowly the map of the city starts re-surfacing in my brain. I lived in Tucson from 2006 to 2010. Now people have moved, grown old, some died, and some are still here. I say over and over to Maureen: "I really love this place, the land, the plants, the houses, the people." Very strong life-long friendships began in my stay in Tucson. When I lived here, I served on the boards of POG and Chax Press; there was a tight community of poet friends, including Frank Parker, Charles Alexander, Cynthia Miller, Tenney Nathanson, Sue Carnahan, Dawn Pendergast, Paul Klinger, Bonnie Jean Michalski, Jake Levine, Tony Luebberman, Laynie Brown, Rodney Phillips, Chris Sawyer, Lisa Anderson Cooper, Lisa Bowden, and others. We curated poetry readings (bringing in poets from around the country) and held reading groups (studying such poets as Barbara Guest, Charles Olson, and Robert Duncan). I also remember sitting Zen with Tenney Nathanson on many Sunday afternoons. (Barb)

Casa Libre on N. 4th Ave, home of many poetry readings and events and once a place where retreating poets could find a space to stay. *(MO)*

In a yoga class this morning at YogaOasis, the teacher was playing Krishna Das music and she talked about how lucky she was to have met him and how he was once nominated for a Grammy. I sit quietly smiling to myself, remembering years back singing kirtan and going on retreats with Krishna Das every week in small groups in NYC at Jivamukti; this was years before he became so famous. My very close yoga pals Lisa Schrempp and Kate Donovan were there, too, and then they both moved to Tucson. When I tell Maureen about it and call up one of his albums on my computer, *Pilgrim Heart*, we both start singing, smiling, and laughing, especially when I show her how we used to dance around the Jiva studio: *Hare ram, hare ram ram ram, hare hare / hare krishna, hare krishna krishna krishna, hare hare* and so on. Now to sing with KD would require going to an auditorium with a crowd of people. But here we are in our little casita singing together. (Barb)

❄

Feb. 12, 2019. Had lovely breakfast at Charles and Cynthia's home. Barbara went to yoga and Cynthia and I sat outside on the brick border soaking up the sunshine. Two hummingbirds flitted about in the olive tree outside their front door. We were so close to them, but they seemed completely unafraid of us. Cynthia said her mother had befriended the hummingbirds for years. Even taking one that had fallen to the ground in bad weather into the house in a tiny soft box, then as the little one came to, setting it outside and free. It seemed like the hummingbirds had grown to trust her mother so much, and now her, that they perched without fear on the branches near us. (MO)

Feb. 14, 2019. In Tucson for a few days before we read, so a nice break in our galloping road trip. We catch up on arrangements for readings ahead, business back home, and laundry. David and Laura Wilk are here on a little respite from East Coast winter and to visit Laura's sister and her husband, who live here. We drive up a little into the hills in Tucson where they have rented an older but beautiful place. Just off a main road we turn onto desert gravel and huge saguaro cactus all around. Suddenly right in front of us a bobcat leisurely strolls across the road, then pauses while we stop the car and stare and shout, "That's a bobcat!" Hardly acknowledging us, the bobcat effortlessly hops up on the adobe wall surrounding a neighboring house. He or she is over and gone before we can get our cameras out. When we pull into David and Laura's for lunch, we are all agog and babbling about seeing the bobcat. We have a sushi lunch out on their southwest-tiled patio. So nice to eat outside even tho the chalky sky is threatening rain. They are such fun to talk to and we chatter on about politics, mothers, folks we know, and our kids. (MO)

On Thursday we have lunch with Maureen's friends **David and Laura Wilk** in the foothills. Before pulling into their drive, I saw a flash of an animal in the road. We pulled up and sat still. At first, I thought it was a coyote, but then Maureen explained it was a bobcat. After watching the big cat climb over the wall into a neighbor's yard, we looked over our shoulders as we walked toward the house. Sitting in the yard, we ate sushi, took selfies, and talked about our lives, the political world, and the lives of poets and friends. I had a long talk with Laura about our mothers and the book I am writing about my mother. We both have had losses in the mother area, and we compared our stories. Laura had a great idea: Jeff Bezos should buy Fox News. I was very happy to meet both David and Laura; both are excited about life, the sky, and the sharp points on the Catalina mountains reaching over the roof of their house. (Barb)

David Wilk, Barbara, Maureen and Laura Wilk

David and I are both from Minnesota and I tell him about my idea for the ten acres of farm homestead my uncle left me there. In honor of my uncle, it would be called "The Bud Phalen Potato Project." David gives me lots of ideas for contacts. My project is to plant potatoes on the ten acres (which has amazing rich black Minnesota soil earth) and then donate them to a food pantry or homeless kitchen in the vicinity. He mentions that there are a number of young people wanting to farm, but don't have the money to start and that through the American Farmland Trust I might find out more about them. He also tells me about a Minnesota food co-op in Minneapolis and a book to find by a food activist titled *Turn Here Sweet Corn*. Now I'm all excited about my potato project again!

Earlier, remembering Laura's gorgeous fabric art and paintings, I ask about her work. Then we digress and she describes a recent revelation she had in Manhattan at the Natural History Museum that changed her way of thinking about things. This leads to a great story that occurred a little after that about an astounding, mind-expanding encounter with a psychic in a séance that has yet to play out.

Back at our casita that night the rain comes down in beneficial torrents. (MO)

❊

After a yoga class this morning, I go over to Karuna's Thai Plate on the corner of Grant and Campbell to wait for **Harriette Hartigan** and her son Zay. All three of us look more weathered than we did eight years ago. Forty-three years ago, Harriette was a hip, long-legged, long-haired photographer. Then she became a midwife-photographer. She snapped the home birth of my daughter and a few years later my son. (While we are chatting, my phone rings. It is my son, Michah, saying hello to everyone.) Zay was just a little boy back then, along with his other two brothers, John and Geordie. Now Zay is a tall cowboy, looking after a ranch, his mother, the woman who owns the ranch, and his daughter. He grew up in a household of mostly boys; now he is surrounded by women. (When I say that, he smiles and taps the table.) Now Harriette is an 80-year-old cowgirl living on a ranch outside of Patagonia. (Barb)

Reflection in Karuna window. *Photo by Harriette Hartigan*

On Friday night we met David and Laura and Laura's sister, Katrina Mangin, and Charles A. at Zemam's Too, an Ethiopian restaurant on Speedway. We devoured authentic cuisine and had a rollicking good time. I tried to use the spongy injera flatbread to scoop the meal but had to resort to a plain old American fork for some of it. I'm sure there is an elegant technique and I have been meaning to learn it. (MO)

❀

Zemam's Too on Speedway Boulevard used to be an old local all-around restaurant, the Garland, but now it is a delicious Ethiopian restaurant. The five us moved around the table chatting with each other, all of us excited talkers with a lot to talk about. When sitting beside Katrina she described the ecology classes she teaches at U of A. Then she told me the story about her husband, Richard Thompson, and how when he was a young grad student, he believed there was a dinosaur in Arizona, and he set out to find one. He scraped and dusted one bone after another and followed the trail—one day he looked up, and low and behold he saw the outline of a huge dinosaur in the rock wall. He contacted the local Desert Museum and now "Sonorasaurus" is officially on display in the Arizona-Sonora Desert Museum. It was named Sonorasaurus Thompsoni after him. (Barb)

Charles and David *(Barb)*

Barbara, Katrina, Charles, David, Maureen, Laura

Feb. 16, 2019. It's Saturday morning and the children are playing in the backyard outside the casita window. Their energy rises in shrieks, hoots, and lyrical hollering. Tonight we read for POG at the Steinfeld Warehouse here in Tucson on the other side of the rail tracks. (MO)

(Barb)

Because I have such a connection with Tucson, it was the perfect place for Maureen and me to take a longer stop. Funny how Tucson has become this spot where so many old friends from Detroit came at one point or another to live. In the morning I met up with Anne Hernandez Urban, the first babysitter for my daughter, and then a lifelong friend. In 1983 she helped me load up my car and then drove to NYC with me, returning to Detroit to help Allen take care of the children until I found a place for us to live. Later she moved to Tucson and helped her husband raise his youngest son. Anne has spent her life working for public health for women and now as a librarian for young children.

At night Maureen and I drove over to the Steinfeld Warehouse for our POG reading. Charles & Cynthia used to have their studio in that building. I remember when I first arrived in Tucson climbing up the back stairs to this rickety warehouse full of artists for a meeting of a Charles Olson reading group. The audience at our reading was mostly poets and many old friends, including Steve Salmoni, Lisa Cooper Anderson, and her husband, Tom Anderson; I was especially happy to give a big hug to a dear friend, Tenney Nathanson; and surprise, surprise, Cynthia Hogue, Mary Rose Larkin, and Joan Larkin were now living in Tucson and were in the audience, and Charles Borkhuis and his wife, Kathy, were passing through town, and there, too. Also, old friends originally from Detroit, Yvonne Reinke and Gary Gibson. Yvonne and Gary took my apartment when I moved from Detroit to NYC in 1983. They still have some records with my name scribbled on the covers. I was especially thankful for Cynthia Miller's introduction, quoting from **Jon Curley's review** of my new novel. While I was reading passages from the novel that took place in part in Tucson, that great Tucson train horn blasted its sound through the space.

Charles Alexander made a beautiful broadside for the reading.

David Wilk recorded our reading and wrote a review in *Writer's Cast: The Voice of Writing.* (Barb)

Photo by David Wilk

The audience at POG was exciting to read to. An eclectic crowd so engaged in language and so fun and easygoing in their pertinent questions at the Q&A after we read. Kelsi Vanada, a former student at Naropa University in Boulder, who now lives here in Tucson, came to hear us. Loved seeing her again and getting to catch up and learn where she is in this expanding world now. And Joan Larkin, wonderful poet and friend from forever, is now in Tucson. It was so great to see her again. She and Bob Hershon, of Hanging Loose Press, coming from Brooklyn, NY, will be reading right here in about a week. Wish we had more time to stay and hear them. David (Wilk) came and recorded us (as did POG) on an impressive, tiny, high-tech device. Surprised and elated to see Charles Borkhuis, who travels around a bit, and, fortuitously for us, happened to be in Tucson. Big shout out to Charles Alexander for an inspired introduction to my reading, and to Cynthia (Miller) who gave a beautiful welcome home introduction, and praise for Barbara. Cynthia also did a fantastic job of setting up a delicious buffet of poetry-reading-style tidbits and drinks. My favorite was the hot apple cider. And, of course, a little wine. And special thanks to Young POG members and volunteers, Cameron especially (who is now on the POG board). Not knowing many folks in Tucson, I so enjoyed meeting the many dedicated poets and writers, spouses and friends that came. Some of us gathered at the Red Garter Saloon after and in the glow of ruby lights the night played on. (MO)

(MO)

David, Maureen, Cynthia, Charles, Lisa, Tom, and Tenney *(Barb)*

The audience in two shots, glued together in Photoshop.
Some of the poets in attendance: Charles Alexander, Cynthia Hogue, Richard
Tavenner, Lisa Martin, David Wilk, Joan Larkin, Maryrose Larkin, Lisa Cooper Anderson,
Kelsi Vanada, Cameron Louie, Charles Borkhuis, and Tenney Nathanson *(Barb)*

Meanwhile, as we travel here on Earth, one of the most successful and enduring feats of interplanetary exploration: NASA's Opportunity rover mission has ended after almost fifteen years exploring the surface of Mars, helping lay the groundwork for NASA's return to the Red Planet. My son, Kyran, and his wife, Nicole, work for NASA at the Jet Propulsion Lab in Pasadena. They have both worked on the Mars rovers and landers, including Curiosity and Opportunity. Nicole is part of the team for the next rover, Mars 2020, and Kyran is on project with InSight, the latest lander. Having such family involvement has heightened my interest in science and space exploration. I felt pretty close to Opportunity as a picture of that little rover has been on my fridge for years. Designed to last just ninety Martian days and travel 1,100 yards (1,000 meters), Opportunity vastly surpassed all expectations in its endurance, scientific value, and longevity. In addition to exceeding its life expectancy by sixty times, the rover traveled more than 28 miles (45 kilometers) by the time it reached its most appropriate final resting spot on Mars—Perseverance Valley. So I felt as tho someone I knew was gone when I read that Opportunity stopped communicating with Earth after a severe Mars-wide dust storm blanketed its location in June, 2018. Since then, JPL engineers tried more than a thousand commands to restore contact, but to no avail. (MO)

❀

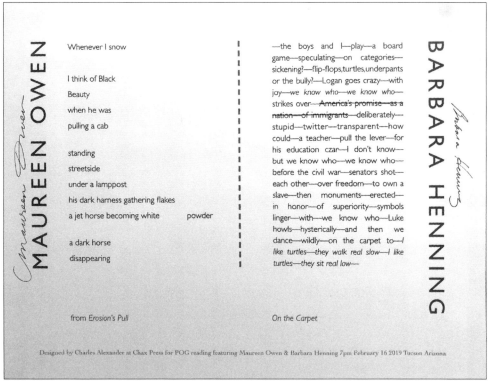

MAUREEN OWEN

Whenever I snow

I think of Black
Beauty
when he was
pulling a cab

standing
streetside
under a lamppost
his dark harness gathering flakes
a jet horse becoming white   powder

a dark horse
disappearing

from *Erosion's Pull*

BARBARA HENNING

—the boys and I—play—a board
game—speculating—on categories—
sickening?—flip-flops,turtles,underpants
or the bully?—Logan goes crazy—with
joy—*we know who*—*we know who*—
strikes over—~~America's promise—as a~~
~~nation—of immigrants~~—deliberately—
stupid—twitter—transparent—how
could—a teacher—pull the lever—for
his education czar—I don't know—
but we know who—we know who—
before the civil war—senators shot—
each other—over freedom—to own a
slave—then monuments—erected—
in honor—of superiority—symbols
linger—with—we know who—Luke
howls—hysterically—and then we
dance—wildly—on the carpet to—*I*
like turtles—they walk real slow—I like
turtles—they sit real low—

On the Carpet

Designed by Charles Alexander at Chax Press for POG reading featuring Maureen Owen & Barbara Henning 7pm February 16 2019 Tucson Arizona

Broadside made by Charles Alexander for our Tucson reading

After we arrived in a friend's place in Phoenix, we received the following
email-poem from David Wilk:

I wrote this for you both, thinking about last night's fun reading:

MAUREEN AND BARBARA COME TO TOWN AND THEN DEPART, BUT NOT BEFORE THE TRAIN PASSES BY WITH A GREETING, CALLING OUT THEIR NAMES

Just about now
the moon is exploding—
happy to see us
as we cross the desert?
first a bobcat calls your name
then a glass of water, we drive

across the Catalinas
and on into California
children are calling
come back, they say
we need your music
to start the day
Bye for now
David

PHOENIX STOP OVER
FEBRUARY 17 - 19, 2019

Maureen and I spent two nights in Phoenix with my close friend, Lisa Schrempp. Lisa is a super maha ashtanga yoga teacher and an Ayurvedic herbalist, cook, and massage therapist. We have been friends for twenty-five years, practicing yoga, cooking, and talking together in NYC, Tucson, and Mysore, India, and even though we now live on opposite sides of the country, we have our cellphones. I have learned so much over the years from Lisa, in her classes, in the kitchen, on the massage table, talking under the moon, all our conversations about how to live a yogic life while we are spinning around inside our souped-up minds and techno-crazy worlds. On our last morning in Phoenix, I woke up with a sore shoulder, so Lisa smoothed, pressed, and re-invigorated all the energy lines in my back, shoulders, and hands with mahanarayana oil. Om Shanti! Shoulder released. Then I taught her a new core practice I had learned from Harkness folks in NYC. I love Lisa and her pal, Bella-dog. (Barb)

https://lisaschrempp.com
(Barb)

En route from Tucson to San Diego we stopped over in Phoenix to visit Barbara's longtime friend, Lisa Schrempp. Lisa teaches Ayurveda and yoga. She and Barbara have known each other for years through yoga classes and travels in India. Her place was big and roomy with life-size folks colorfully painted on the chairs around her table. She was the perfect host, making us unique dinners from her Ayurveda cookbook. I was intrigued and picked up a few pointers from her: black seeds, turmeric in scrambled eggs, tumis, and that mushrooms are good for the immune system and the lungs. She brewed us homemade healing teas and created exotic desserts. The two nights we were there, I joined her and her Doberman Pinscher, Bella, for their nightly walk. We headed out both nights under a moon coming to full, a grand super moon expected in a night or two. Both eves the sky was crisp and clear, and hosts of stars binged in the dark desert heavens over us. We strode along for a few blocks through her neighborhood then came to a green belt area with a little lake and a lighted, wild, double water fountain spraying, glistening high and away. Unleashed, Bella took off like a rocket and shot far out of sight into the dark until all we could see was a tiny silhouette of her perked ears and sleek shape sprinting the water's edge. I so enjoyed meeting Lisa and our chats as we trekked into the brisk, invigorating desert airs. (MO)

(Barb)

Onward to San Diego

February 20, 2019

Today we left our hotel room at Quality Inn in Blythe, California, just over the border from Arizona, and quickly we were on the two-lane Highway 78 heading toward San Diego. We thought we had three hundred miles to travel and were relieved to discover it was only 215 miles. Zoom. Highway 78 was an ever-transforming panorama of different vistas, from green farmland to desert to plains of white sand with beach folks arriving in campers and plowing through the terrain in their various vehicles. As we went along, I figured out a way to mount my cell and take photos as I was driving, shifting, and drinking water. Maureen must have pushed her phantom brake foot into the floor more than a few times as I played with the camera on the dashboard, but she never screamed. Finally, I goofed up enough that it was clear I had to stop driving and turn over the wheel. On US 8, it was desert again until the mountains started, miles and miles of rock-pile mountains. Finally, we started moving downward back to sea level and San Diego. Our ears were popping. In North Park, we unlocked the door to a little three-room house. By now, we are used to unpacking and repacking and unpacking and settling into a new environment. At home for three nights and two readings at D.G. Wills Books and at Cal State San Marcos. Then off we will go to LA. (Barb)

✤

We travel from Blythe, CA, to San Diego on I-10 West, then take 78 West, the most scenic road we've traveled so far. We drive up & down

75

the short hills and dips, yellow desert flowers fill the sides of the highway. Then, still desert, but greener with bushes and scrub trees that seem to be getting water from somewhere, a really beautiful landscape. A hawk lifts off over us. A range of crumpled looking mountains encircle us. And the scene keeps changing. A huge quarry has plateaued and terraced several mountains to our right. Then just after leaving Glamis and before Brawley, we see pure white peaks ahead of us. Highway 78 goes right through the Imperial Sand Dunes. So vast! Incredible stretches of dunes, a tawny, smooth, lumbering velvet that surrounds us as we drive snapping photos. We seem to be engulfed in their giant mounds forever, then abruptly their wonder ends and we are back in sage and rambling desert. Now we begin to see more small farms where the farmers drive simple, older style John Deere tractors, not the behemoth rigs of the giant co-op farms in the Midwest. A canal of blue water flows between the field edge and the road. Then a cattle lot with what appears to be hundreds of Holsteins grouped in smaller numbers in separate pens. A grim, dismal sight to see them shut up in small pens with the wide land around them teasing freedom. Then irrigated crops, small farms with goats and a large herd of sheep. On I-8 West up into the mountains and a light drizzle and down into San Diego where traffic multiplies and roars. We find our casita in a charming cottage type neighborhood and park our car on the acute angle driveway hoping it won't roll away. (MO)

Poison glimmering
in the sun *(Barb)*

Our home for three nights

San Marcos & La Jolla
February 21 - 22, 2019

Feb. 21, 2019. I love this little house. A long living room/kitchen, the size of my studio, then alongside it another strip of two bedrooms with a bath in between. High ceilings. That is the house. A small house, but big enough for someone like me to live in. And the neighborhood is mellow. Small southwestern houses in California pastels. (Barb)

❊

I called my mom to wish her happy birthday. She's ninety-six today! Back in Denver my son and my brother are planning a birthday party. My brother is baking the cake. (MO)

(MO)

It was cold in San Diego today and it seemed to never stop raining. We took out our winter coats and put the address of Pizza Nova in San Marcos into our GPS. The GPS voice directed us from one freeway to another. It was hailing, then pouring rain, then a freeway with nine lanes, three HOV and six right beside it, all the cars going eighty miles per hour with a sixty-five max. The GPS instructions were not that clear and a bit delayed with three lane ramps, each lane heading somewhere else. Out of fear, we got off the freeway and disobeyed our instructions taking regular streets until we were near the campus and at the restaurant where we were to meet Mark Wallace and his student poet-writers, Beth Phung, Lineth Velasco, Laura Jefchak, Nicole Barnes, and Mike Thomas. We chatted for an hour or so and then followed the students, driving to the campus. On campus, we were greeted by a big lecture hall full of students for the first reading this year of "The Community and World Series." Over the years Mark has brought many poets to San Marcos; this is my second trip here. He introduced both of us, talking about the commonalities in our writing. (Barb)

Here's Mark introduction:

It's not often that I introduce two people with one introduction, but I'm going to try, so that my own comments don't take much time away from these two writers who I am very pleased to be able to welcome to Cal State San Marcos. When I think about what their work has in common, I find a lot. Maybe foremost is openness to experience, the idea that to be a writer is to engage oneself in the whole range of experiences that are involved in being human. Both Barbara Henning and Maureen Owen write work that is very attuned to actual moments of living, that shows readers the value of noticing, of responding, of interacting. Both of them do those things through writing that is also clear about what it means to struggle, to not be able to take safety or possibility or love or trust or anything for granted, to know that a person has to always be working *towards* a thing to make it so. They are both brave writers, willing to tell the truth about people and experience and the worlds of politics and culture on a planet that is now itself at risk from what people, all of us, are doing with it and to it. To me personally, what's perhaps most important when I read their work, is that the world seems a bigger place, both in its wonders and in its dangers, and I feel drawn outside of the small, well-defended boundaries of myself and into a recognition that living is a kind of grand strangeness. Please welcome Barbara Henning and Maureen Owen.

Mark Wallace
(Barb)

After our reading, students gathered around us asking questions. I read some passages from *Just Like That*, as well as poetry. In the beginning of the novel, the narrator tells a story about her Italian boyfriend, when she was eighteen years old; his name is Vinny. A student asked me afterward if I was Italian. "No, but I grew up in an Italian-American community, and I did have an Italian boyfriend when I was young." Smile. He then announced that he could relate to the story and his name was Vinny. We both laughed.

I first came to know Mark when he was a grad student in the Buffalo Poetics Program. He and Kristen Prevellet were editing Leave Books and they published a sequence of my poems, *The Passion of Signs*. Then as years passed, we crisscrossed the country, meeting at readings in NYC, Tucson, and Washington DC. (He taught at George Washington

University before moving to California). I remember a memorable visit to Tucson in 2009 when I took Mark and K. Lorraine Graham to the Desert Museum. Besides having written many books of poetry and fiction, **Mark Wallace** also reviews and writes about poetics.

Mark gave us each a copy of *The End of America: Book Three*. In *Across the Margin* (website), the editor comments on Book 11:

> *Mark Wallace's revelatory poetry trenchantly captures what it feels like to be an awake self dealing with the crumbling infrastructure of country and culture. The often mind-numbing contradictions of our current American moment disjunctively flow into the soaring half-truths of how we attempt to make sense of them, the poet knowing full well that "A word does not/ create freedom."*

When we left San Marcos, the freeways were even more challenging in the dark, with the rain, and so many cars, going so fast in all those lanes. Up ahead we could see them snaking toward us and then away. (Barb)

❖

Here in SD we drove on a six-lane freeway in mega traffic through heavy rain and then small, iced water hail to San Marcos. We met Professor Mark Wallace and five of his students at Pizza Nova before our reading. It was fun and inspiring to hear what the students are doing and thinking here. One of Mark's students, Beth Phung, gave me some new pointers on how to navigate Instagram. The students formed a caravan out of the parking lot at Pizza Nova to lead us to a hard-to-find lot on the campus for the reading. The chilling rain continued. Cold does seem to be our sidekick as we travel.

We read to a full gathering of students both from Mark's class and from a number of the creative writing classes at Cal State San Marcos. Afterward we had an informal Q&A with students just coming up to each of us directly with queries on our works and our writing processes. They were all such earnest people and a joy to discuss poetics with. Laura

Jefchak was there, a student and reporter for the university newspaper, doing an article on us for the *Cougar Chronicle*. (MO)

Photo by Lineth Velasco

The Community and World Literary Series Presents:

Barbara Henning and Maureen Owen

Thursday, February 21, 7 p.m.
Markstein Hall 125
California State University, San Marcos

Poet and fiction writer Barbara Henning was born in Detroit, Michigan. Her books of poems include *Smoking in the Twilight Bar*, *A Swift Passage*, *Cities and Memory*, *My Autobiography*, *Detective Sentences* and *Love Makes Thinking Dark*. She is also the author of four novels, *Just Like That* (Spuyten Duyvil, 2018), *Thirty Miles to Rosebud, You Me and the Insects,* and *Black Lace*. A long-time yoga practitioner, having lived and studied in Mysore, India with Shankaranarayana Jois, she brings this knowledge and discipline to her writing and her teaching.

Maureen Owen is a poet, editor and publisher currently living in Denver, CO. She is the author of eleven books of poetry, most recently *Edges of Water* from Chax Press. Her title *Erosion's Pull* from Coffee House Press was a finalist for the Colorado Book Award and the Balcones Poetry Prize. Her collection *American Rush: Selected Poems* was a finalist for the L.A. Times Book Prize and her work *AE (Amelia Earhart)* was a recipient of the Before Columbus American Book Award. Her work has been included in several anthologies including *Moving Borders: Three Decades of Innovative Writing By Women*. She served as program coordinator at The St. Mark's Poetry Project in New York for a famously lengthly time.

Feb. 22, 2019. We drove to La Jolla to read at D.G. Wills Books. Tucked in on an active street amid restaurants and shops, Dennis Wills's bookstore is a one-of-a-kind treasure house of a multitude of volumes. I immediately wanted to be living down the block so I could come there every day and linger over the titles and various art objects placed about. From books on magic to a poetry section that makes one's heart flutter, the shelves go at every angle to profit every bit of space in what is not that many square feet. Dennis had our books ordered and out for sale and talked about the microphone that had been used by a host of poets and writers over the many years of readings at the store. When I read, I thought of that sacredness as my words flowed out into it. We read to an intimate gathering that included two young women students who had driven all the way from Cal State San Marcos, as they had not been able to come to our reading there last night. My dear friends Rayna Bailey and Mike Leboffe came, and Jerome Rothenberg and his wife, Diane, and Diane's sister, who is visiting from New Jersey. We met Steve Simpson, who has been deep in the poetry community over many years and had great stories of time spent with folks we both knew. Steve is a collector of printed broadsides and broadsides of poems written out by the poet's own hand (often only one or two copies of these made). Definitely contact him if you'd be interested in a broadside from now and dating back to the early Beats. Dennis told me that the parents of Colorado's new governor, Jared Polis, live in La Jolla and he has been longtime good friends with them. They come to the bookstore often. Another small world moment, since I live in Denver now where Jared Polis has just been elected our governor. After we read, we took some Q&A and signed books and pamphlets. Then we joined the Rothenbergs at an elaborate fish restaurant, El Pescador, over a block and up the street a couple more. I mention that one of the best things about our road tour is visiting and connecting with the folks in the various poetry communities we read at. Jerome elaborates wisely that, yes, there is an extended poetry network that exists and that we are all members. Like being members of an invisible organization, we can all find each other wherever we go. (MO)

Dennis Wills
(Barb)

At 5 p.m. we packed up our books and set the GPS for D.G. Wills Books in La Jolla. Only fifteen miles but again swerving wildly around on the six-lane wide freeways. I always thought of California as more laid back than NYC, but to tell you the truth, NYC seems Old World and California, well, she is flying off the globe. The bookstore was packed with old and new books in the windows and angling here and there, nooks and crannies with shelves of books. The books are side-by-side to all kinds of heavy antique tools and old manual typewriters. I told the owner Dennis Wills a story about how my children's father collected similar things; once when the city was rebuilding the Brooklyn Bridge, he picked up several very heavy large pieces of metal and bolts from the old bridge. They are now sitting in my son's apartment. Dennis has been hosting writers in his bookstore for years; he has a very warm and welcoming, laidback presence. He explained to us that we were speaking into the same mic as Maureen Dowd, Michael McClure, Francoise Gilot, Gore Vidal, Gary Snyder, and Allen Ginsberg. Then home on the highway of highways ripping over the hills back to North Park, where we looked over photos, put together some text, packed up to head to LA in the morning, and put our bodies to rest. (Barb)

Photos by Steve Simpson and DG Wills

Barb, Jerome and Diane Rothenberg, Diane's sister, Maureen

Colorado poet

MAUREEN OWEN

reads from her book EDGES of WATER
and New York poet

BARBARA HENNING

reads from her book A DAY LIKE TODAY

Friday, February 22, 7PM, 2019

Maureen Owen, former editor and chief of *Telephone Magazine* and Telephone Book, is the author of eleven books of poetry, most recently *Edges of Water* from Chax Press. Her title *Erosion's Pull* from Coffee House Press was a finalist for the Colorado Book Award and the Balcones Poetry Prize. Her collection *American Rush: Selected Poems* was a finalist for the L.A. Times Book Prize and her work *AE(Amelia Earhart)*was a recipient of the prestigious Before Columbus American Book Award. She has most recently published work in *Dispatches, Positive Magnets #5, Resist much/Obey Little, The Denver Quarterly, Vanitas, New American Writing,* and *Bombay Gin.* Her awards include grants from the Foundation for Contemporary Arts, the Fund for Poetry and a Poetry Fellowship from the National Endowment for the Arts. She has taught at Naropa University and served as editor-in-chief of Naropa's on-line zine *not enough night.*

Barbara Henning is the author of four novels, seven collections of poetry, four chapbooks and a series of photo-poem pamphlets. Lewis Warsh published her first book of poems with United Artists, *Smoking in the Twilight Bar.* Subsequent poetry collections include *A Day Like Today, A Swift Passage, Cities and Memory, My Autobiography, Detective Sentences, Love Makes Thinking Dark.* Her novels include *Just Like That, Thirty Miles to Rosebud, You Me and the Insects,* and *Black Lace.* Between 2003 and 2014, she published limited editions of a series of artist pamphlets (16), combining photography and poetry. Poems from her current poetic project *Digigrams* have been published in several journals, including *Dispatches, Talisman, The Brooklyn Rail, Journal of Poetics Research, Posit* and *Recluse.*
Henning is the editor of a book of interviews, *Looking Up Harryette Mullen,* and *The Selected Prose of Bobbie Louise Hawkins.* She was also the editor of the poetry/art journal, *Long News: In the Short Century* (1990-1995). As a long-time yoga practitioner, having lived and studied in Mysore, India with Shankaranarayana Jois, she brings this knowledge and discipline to her writing and her teaching at Naropa University (2006-14), University of Arizona (2006-2009), and Long Island University in Brooklyn, where she is Professor Emerita.

D.G. WILLS BOOKS

7461 Girard Avenue, La Jolla, (858) 456-1800
www.dgwillsbooks.com

VENICE

FEBRUARY 22 - 24, 2019

We arrived in Venice, California, in early afternoon at the Breeze Suites right on the beach. We unpacked the car and Barbara went to park it in a nearby lot. As I lugged our bags into our room, I could see, through the almost floor to ceiling windows facing the ocean, a Mardi Gras style parade coming up the boardwalk. People in all manner of wild costume came carrying a huge banner that proclaimed, "I Love Venice." Singing and chanting with drinks in some hands, walking and riding decorated bikes and scooters, they were a jubilant welcome. I love the ocean especially the Pacific, so I had to pause even after they passed and look out on the light sand and the two white sailboats out on the blue water. The elevation here is ten feet and having the Pacific a short stroll from the door made me utterly happy.

Almost immediately, we went down to the street to meet Harryette Mullen, terrific poet and writer, who lives in LA, and who was picking us up for a late lunch. She drove us to a busy, happening restaurant, Café Gratitude, where we had a lot of fun mixed with serious talking and eating. (MO)

❋

We left San Diego in the morning of the 23rd and stopped in a café to write. We were a bit concerned that we might get to the Venice Breeze Suites too early to check in and there is no parking there, so we stalled in the café. Then we drove to LA. It was Saturday so the highways were not too jammed. We made one wrong turn, but still made it there at 1:15 p.m., quickly unloaded our things and went downstairs, stashed the car in a public lot, and watched Venice beach folks dancing, singing, and trotting down the boardwalk. At 2 p.m. Harryette Mullen picked us up for lunch and we went to Café Gratitude, a vegan restaurant, arranged because of my diet preferences. Thank you, Harryette and Maureen.

Then at night Maureen and I decided to attend a reading at Beyond Baroque. **Brenda Hillman** was scheduled to read with two others. I admire Brenda's writing and was easily coaxed out of my burrowing-into-nighttime idea. We took a cab and it was worth it. Brenda read from her new book, *Extra Hidden Life*. I was moved by her poems dedicated to C.D. Wright. I'm now reading a few of her poems every night before bed. Probably I'll include some of these in the class I am teaching at the Poet's House in April on "Dedications, Portraits & Elegies." Harryette was at the reading and she drove us home. Enroute, we cut down the alleys to the hotel, and I noticed lots of people sleeping outside in tents or in corners. Harryette told us a story about an advocate for the homeless in LA, Andy Bales, who was working with the homeless and picked up a terrible skid-row disease; his foot and part of his leg had to be amputated. According to Harryette, he continues to work with the homeless and his experience has led to some positive changes in the way LA is dealing with the homeless. (Barb)

❀

That evening we went to Beyond Baroque to hear Brenda Hillman, Sara Mumolo & Vanessa Angelica Villareal read their work. Sara is the author of *Mortar* from Omnidawn and Vanessa is the author of the poetry collection *Beast Meridian*. Brenda read from her latest book, *Extra Hidden Life, Among the Days*. Their words and energy filled the theater space. I felt lucky to be in the audience. This was my intro to Sara and Vanessa's work, but I have been a longtime fan of Brenda Hillman's and it was especially meaningful to see her in person again and say hello. (MO)

(MO)

On Sunday the 24th, after yoga, we asked the desk clerk for breakfast place suggestions and he highly praised the Fig Tree Café just a ways up the boardwalk. The sun was shining, and we began to warm up from the chilly weather that has accompanied us on our travels. As we ate, I had a dish called the Lulu, also recommended by the desk clerk, and a singer named Dale serenaded the boardwalk and our table with covers from Johnny Cash, Jim Morrison, Janis Joplin, Walt Disney, U2, and the Beach Boys. He and his guitar appeared to have been at their gig a long time. We wished the best for him and donated. More people, bikes, scooters, and skateboards joined walkers and joggers on the paved beach path and boardwalk, as we headed back to prepare for our reading. (MO)

❋

In the morning we walked the beach. Even though it was not swimming weather, there were crowds of people out celebrating sunshine and sand. In the afternoon we went over to Beyond Baroque to read. Unfortunately, we did not realize that we had scheduled our reading on the same day as the Oscars, and in LA even poets stay home and tune in. So it was a small audience, but a very special audience. In the dark as I was reading, I could sense a few people slipping in and settling down in the theater seats. It was wonderful to read for Harryette Mullen, Dale Herd, Bill Mohr, and the others. We went out to eat later with Dale and Harryette. Of course, I love Harryette's writing; the book of interviews I did with her, **Looking Up Harryette Mullen** (along with her poems in *Sleeping with the Dictionary),* has probably inspired a lot of young poets to experiment with language. I'm also an admirer of **Dale Herd's stories**. We have been in correspondence for quite some time, and I include his stories in every class I teach on tiny fictions. Check out his new collection: *Empty Pockets: New and Selected Stories* (Coffee House). Overall it was a poetically inspiring two days in LA. (Barb)

❀

We left our car in the parking lot and took a cab to Beyond Baroque. Richard Modiano instructed us on the finely tuned pickup of the microphone, and the director at BB, Quentin Ring, introduced us to a small but engaging audience. After the reading we had a great time talking to Dale Herd, astoundingly wonderful short story writer, and Bill Mohr, who David Wilk had told about our reading. We hung out in the fine little bookstore there with Harryette, Quentin, Dale, Bill, and Emmitt, who manages the bookstore. Then we went out for a bite with Harryette and Dale. I was so delighted to see Dale who I'd met years ago at the Poetry Project at St. Mark's and have been a fan ever since. It was very special to have him in the audience. Thanks to Quentin Ring, Richard Modiano, and Emmett Conklin for setting up the reading and selling the books. (MO)

Quentin Ring *(Barb)*

Bill Mohr with Maureen
(Barb)

Harryette, Barbara, Dale, Maureen. *Photo by Quentin Ring*

Back in the apartment, my shoulder was hurting a lot, some pinched nerve. The woman at the desk found a massage center in Venice still open and they made an appointment for me. I took a cab and a young Chinese woman worked on my shoulder for an hour. She told me that a bad spirit had woven itself into my neck under my skull and she had never seen anything like it before. She huffed and pressed into the acupuncture points and released the spirit. Then she carefully undid every knot in my shoulder girdle. For some reason on this trip, I lost my sense of alignment—maybe from not walking enough, driving so much, and talking so much (usually I'm alone); she was incredibly helpful. I was concerned about her at the end though, because she was tense about her next client, a man, and it was kind of late by then, 9 p.m. I asked her why she was working so late and she said, "I need the money."

On Monday, we woke up, had breakfast, I did my yoga practice. Then we started driving out of LA, on 101 North to Paso Robles where we were stopping for the night. The mountains and the Pacific were awesome. (Barb)

❉

I wake up early and look out on the boardwalk. Last night a masterful drumming session went on till about 10 p.m. continuing the ambiance of the unique, but sometimes less than glamorous, lifestyles here on the beach. Now it's Monday morning quiet and a slightly pale light flutters over the scene. A young woman on a skateboard, a cup of coffee in her hand, glides up the paved beach path that weaves along the boardwalk. Some joggers, a fellow with a backpack, sipping coffee as he steers his bike by a couple of old timers sitting on the benches. The old timers bent forward, look tired and worn, probably having spent the night in a makeshift nearby. We pack up our little traveling caravan and head out on 101 North to Paso Robles, the first leg of our drive to San Francisco. The 101 follows along the ocean through green, lush hills. It's truly a gorgeous drive. When we want to switch drivers and need to stretch our legs, we take a side road down to the beach areas and get out to stretch. When we look down over the cliff edge, we see a campground of RVs. They could have been camping or living in that perfect spot. We wonder if one could just pull in there and park for free. It almost looks like it. As we drive further, we see a long line of RVs parked right alongside the road. One after another, with spaces to park their cars and all. (MO)

(Barb)

SAN FRANCISCO & BERKELEY
FEBRUARY 26 - MARCH 1, 2019

Feb. 26, 2019. As we pulled out of the La Quinta Inn heading to Paso Robles, we passed a small pen with life-size metal replicas of two giraffes looking so inquisitively at the highway that it was hard to believe they weren't real. The 101 North continued through rolling green with hills and hills of grapevines in dormant winter stage. This is wine country. Soon after we arrived yesterday, La Quinta had wine tastings at round marble tables in an elegant section of their lobby. While we drove along, we talked a bit about short stories, and Barbara told me the plots of several of the stories she assigns to the students in her classes. Hawthorne, Carver, Neale Hurston, Melville, Faulkner, it makes me want to take her class. In Salinas we saw a sign on an art center or music studio that said Roaring Mice. We think we can find chai and lattes here as Salinas is home to Hartnell College and those are the brews of student life. As we got closer to our Airbnb in Berkeley the traffic began to magnify. Soon we were bumper-to-bumper, stopping and starting, and the rains began to pour. Cars and trucks turning in other lanes sprayed us with water. Barbara navigated while I drove. At last we arrived and unpacked as quickly as possible in the rain. Our new temporary quarters were roomy and we found a home-baked lemon pound cake in the fridge with a sweet note from the owners. A little wet and cold, it was teatime.

I called my mom. My brother, who had been with her for a week, was going home to Santa Rosa in the morning and her caregiver had returned. My brother lives not too far from where we will be staying for our reading in Sebastopol, and they both voiced concern as major flooding was going on in that area with all the rains. Some places and a town had already been evacuated. I emailed our hosts, Pat Nolan and Gail King, to see if they were threatened by the rising Russian River. We hoped they hadn't been evacuated.

Our quarters were probably a former storefront and right on the Martin Luther King, Jr. Boulevard. Lots of traffic, which amplified by the rains, made roaring swishes in the night. The hot water was heated by a flash water heater that went on loudly when we used hot water. But all the noises were friendly and we liked this place. (MO)

❋

We arrived at our rental in Berkeley, a two-bedroom small duplex that is perfect. A refrigerator, stove, and a big dining room table where Maureen and I set up with our computers to write. So far on this trip, between driving, blogging, reading at events, and going to the laundromat, I have read, responded to, and critiqued over seventy-five poems or short-short fictions by online students. Sort of moody lately. Missing being home. Every so often Maureen and I look over at each other and say: "I can't believe it. We actually did this. Here we are already near the end of our trip." (Barb)

❋

Pat Nolan reported from the flood zone along the Russian River:
> Hi Maureen. We are doing fine and not among the evacuees. And we still have power! We will be high and dry through it all. The river is expected to crest at 46.1 feet (that .1 makes a difference). If you saw the sat pic of the storm, it's like a fire hose aimed directly at Sonoma County. Anyway, tomorrow's precipitation will determine if the predicted crest holds. At 46 feet I might get a little water (inches) in my studio downstairs. Unlike floods back east this one will be gone by Friday morning. The roads should be passable by then as well. I will update you tomorrow once I have a better idea on how all this'll shake out. (MO)

❋

Feb. 27, 2019. This morning I called Diane di Prima to make sure she was still up for a visit. She had a cold and wanted to make sure that we were not worried about catching it. I reassured her that we were okay. When I asked if she wanted anything, she said, no, she wanted many things, but it wasn't feasible at this time. We put the address of the Jewish Home for the Aged into our GPS and set out for San Francisco over the Bay Bridge. About thirteen miles and it took an hour, most of the time spent in a traffic jam on I-80 waiting to go over the bridge. (Barb)

(MO)

I had not seen Diane since October 2010 when I introduced her at the Living Theater and when she was also reading at CUNY and at the Bowery Poetry Club. See below photo I took of her at the Bowery with David Henderson. And another fuzzy photo Dumisani Kambi-Shamba took of Diane and me at the Living Theater. Ten years later Diane is no longer on oxygen, but she is suffering from a number of problems, most recently trouble with her knee. Aging is difficult, I think, already feeling it in my own skeleton. ("All I can say about old age is Oy!" Norma Cole writes in a recent email.) Even so, Diane is very light in spirit, still working on her projects and meeting with students. Sheppard comes every evening for several hours and they work together; they have been together for over forty years. Diane has a new book coming soon from City Lights, writings never before published from the '60s, *Spring and Autumn Annals: A Celebration of the Seasons for Freddie.* (Barb)

Diane di Prima and
David Henderson

Diane and Barbara

Luckily, we left early as traffic was backed up getting across the Bay Bridge. Still sprinkling rain, but sun peeking in and out occasionally.

It was an honor and privilege to spend some time with Diane. Her room had stacks of books, orchids on the windowsill, and prayer flags over a shrine to her Tibetan Buddhist teacher. Facing her bed, a bulletin board had cut-out pics, photos, and a cover shot of her upcoming title, *Spring & Autumn Annals* from City Lights. The image is a snapshot of her hanging clothes on a New York City rooftop around 1963. I have a longtime attachment to clothes hanging on a line. There is something so human and beautiful in clothes-pinned laundry drying in the open sun and air. Clean many colored fabrics, a wash fluttering and blowing in the breeze. Diane's writing, raising children, making revolutionary change, getting things done, a leader of women, are all there in that cover shot. As she said when we were leaving to continue our Poets on the Road readings, "Onward, onward to the sun!" Her remarkable spirit was everywhere in the room as we talked. (MO)

(Barb)

Wouldn't it be great if aged care facilities could offer learning from the ancient Ayurvedic herbalists? Diane has many friends and her own knowledge of herbs and she is lucky for that. In South India, many Indians take an oil bath once a week to keep flexible (applying oil to every part of the body). There is also an herbal oil that helps with pain (and joint lubrication), mahanarayana. I order a small bottle from Banyan and send it to Diane. Maybe it will help with her knee. And I promise myself to start this routine again, every week when I am back in Brooklyn.

Below is the poem that Diane gave me once for a collection of prose poems I was using for my grad courses, and her process note. Soon this poem will be included in a book Spuyten Duyvil is publishing, *Prompt Book: Experiments for Writing Poetry and Fiction*. (Barb)

WISTERIA LIGHT
by Diane di Prima

In the early days of eternity when none of us was naked as yet, and a good thing too, I opted to plaster the back stairs. Not that the stairs wanted to be plastered, but I was certain that was the only way the billiard table would fit. Workmen dropped hammers here & there. You were vacuuming, by god, though the plaster wasn't dry, as if you were going to get an A for neatness. There were two slots in this greeting card, a kind of microchip it was, with Franz Kline wiring, not that we thought then that black & white would be a problem even for the moon. Our returning to the same haven as uncertain as coming out each time in a different one. No one distinguished between the blessed & the unblessed, no immortals had immigrated here for some time. I wanted to order wisteria, something to mitigate the light in those canyons. When you wisely pointed out it wouldn't grow there, I thought to murder you with the pail with which you were mopping the windows. I clearly saw brick walls, the red mellowing to yellow, or brown shingle shadowed with the ancient vines. I wanted none of those we had invited, whoever they were. Or the flat light they loved. I saw that clearly. Return to the present was an unhappy business, saturated as it was with murdered swallows. I Vesperi Siciliani slid into one slot, and I was afraid Pagliacci would find the other. And there we would be, like the king who drives his chariot around & around in that tiny courtyard, circles of paving stones without even a pear tree. Stuck as a crow on a telephone pole, once you've seen it, the pole is never again empty, there's always a crow, black in your mind's eye in front of the white sky before sunrise.

❃

Back in Berkeley we got a second flood report from Pat:

> Hi Maureen, spent most of the morning clearing out my studio accompanied with exclamations of "That's where I put that!" and "Why did I keep that?" Anyway watching the creek back up into our back yard slowly (a kind of water torture) but surely. With two more feet to go, the carpet in my studio will get wet but that's about all. . . . So we visit with the neighbors in their rain gear and waders and talk of floods from years past.

Outside our on-the-street door, cars were still swishing through rainy streets. Then a further update from Pat:

> Some sporadic showers overnight but sunshine tomorrow. River expected to crest at 45.5 around 11 p.m. Unfortunately, the carpet did get wet, but as I predicted about three inches. We'll rip that out in the weeks to come. I like the idea of tile so maybe we'll go with that. The neighborhood is flooded in, but the road out will be passable by midday. Right around the time you're talking to Steve's class. (MO)

❃

Feb. 28, 2019. In the morning, we headed to San Francisco over the Bay Bridge and met Steve Dickison at Café Rosso across from the Humanities Building at San Francisco State University. Then he took us to the Poetry Center where we looked at the vast library and signed many of our books for Steve and the center. We then moved on to Steve's classroom for the reading. We were especially happy when Norma Cole and Susan Gevirtz came to the class to hear us read. (Barb/MO)

Steve Dickinson Introducing *(MO)*

Norma Cole, Susan Gevirtz, Steve Dickison *(Barb)*

The students had already read and discussed the poems in our pamphlet. We both read from the pamphlet. Maureen also read from *Erosion's Pull* and *Edges of Water*; and Barbara read from her novel, *Just Like That*, and from *A Day Like Today*. Then we answered questions from the students. Some of their questions were about Maureen's titles, why we use space and punctuation the way we do, where we get our ideas from, how to get published, and how one includes political ideas in poems. Afterward, we signed books; then we sat outside at Rosso and ate sandwiches before heading back to Berkeley. (Barb/MO)

(Barb/MO)

That night after a brief rest, we drove over to Moe's Books on Telegraph Avenue. Joyce Jenkins and Richard Silberg from **Poetry Flash** arrived with boxes of our books that they put on display. Richard introduced us with a lively take on our poems in the *Poets on the Road* pamphlet. We were especially happy to read for Steve Emerson and his wife Gayle, Alan Bernheimer, and Ted Pearson, among others. See link in Appendix D for **Moe's announcement** for our reading. (Barb/MO)

Richard Silberg introducing

Alan Bernheimer

(Barb)

Alan Bernheimer's head shots

MO & Joyce Jenkins *(Barb)*

Joyce reminded me that she had lived in Detroit in the '70s. As we talked, we discovered that we were both in fact living in the Cass Corridor a few doors away from each other and we had hung out in the same clubs, Alvin's and Cobb's Corner Bar. We surely must have known some of the same people and passed each other on the street. We might have sat across from each other on Sundays in the café in the Art Institute, reading *The Times* and drinking coffee. (Barb)

❊

So enjoyed talking to poet friends I hadn't seen in a while. A nice surprise was meeting Steve Emerson's wife, Gayle, who like myself grew up on a farm out on the Midwest prairies. She's from North Dakota and I'm from Minnesota. We had such similar memories of mothers and grandmothers tending and depending on big gardens and canning produce to make it through the winter. We talked about living far out of town in those remote places and being closely knit with family. Our growing-up lives seemed like mirrors of each other. (MO)

Mar. 1, 2019. Friday morning after we packed up, we met **Gloria Frym** for brunch in Berkeley. Great to see her again! She couldn't come to our reading at Moe's the night before because it was her birthday and friends were taking her out. The restaurant she was taking us to, Bette's Oceanview Diner, no longer had an ocean view as over the years many buildings rose up between it and the sea. But it was certainly popular, too popular, with a half hour wait, so we went around the corner to another café for our brunch. We chatted variously and then a lot about teaching creative writing in today's economy. Gloria gave us each a copy of her book, *The True Patriot*, from Spuyten Duyvil, and we gave her copies of our books and our *Poets on the Road* pamphlet. Then hugs and we were off. There was an email from Pat Nolan and Gail King, our hosts, that roads might be blocked because of the rain and floods. (MO)

Maureen, Barb, and Gloria

SEBASTOPOL & BEYOND

MARCH 2 - 8, 2019

Mar. 2, 2019. Pat and Gail decided to meet us at a place outside the flooded area. Pat and I have been friends since I first met him years ago when he came to read in NYC at the St. Mark's Poetry Project. I have a treasured collection of his woodblock prints and handmade books he has sent me over the years. And of his collections of the renga writings he, Keith Abbott, Michael Sowl, and I have collaborated on over the years. The last time I visited Pat and Gail, my mother and I had driven down from my brother's place near Santa Rosa. We had a magical time, walking by the then peaceful Russian River and sitting in the sunshine chatting. It was a visit my mother often talks about remembering them both so fondly. My longtime dear friend, Sandy Berrigan, came down from her place in Albion for our reading in Sebastopol and was staying with Nancy Packard, a longtime friend of hers, nearby. So Nancy's became our rendezvous point. Sandy is a poet and also a writer of rengas, a Japanese collaborative form, with one in progress starring herself, Pat, Elinor Nauen, and myself. Nancy's house was full of music and musical instruments. We thoroughly enjoyed meeting her. (MO)

❀

Pat Nolan and Gail King live in a little enclave in Monte Rio, a village alongside the Russian River, a river that recently overflowed, damaging and destroying lots of houses. Twenty years ago, their house was devastated by a flood and afterward they had the house lifted up eight feet above the ground. This time, their basement was flooded, and they only lost some furniture and a carpet. Many of the people in the community were much harder hit. Mud covered the roads and big piles of ruined furniture were scattered along the roadside. We stayed with Gail and Pat for three nights. Three days and nights full of talking about poetry and poets. Sandy Berrigan joined us on Saturday. We ate walnuts from the tree outside their window, played a renku poetry game Pat and a friend had invented, ate tamales and lentil soup, looked at Pat's woodblock art and magazines and books he had published over the years. We all gifted each other copies of our books. It was very comfortable staying with Pat and Gail, almost as if I had known them my whole life. (Barb)

Gail, Pat, Sandy, Barb *(MO)*

Besides being a prolific writer, editor, and publisher, **Pat Nolan** was also a dispatcher for the fire department. **Gail King** is a substitute teacher and a school bus driver. She feeds a tribe of feral cats who camp out under their cars and in baskets on their porch and under the house. When I opened the door to go outside, they scattered. Whoosh! Two somewhat more domestic cats live inside. They have a beautiful walnut tree on their property and the houses in their enclave are surrounded by tall redwood pines. Gail told me that they are young trees; I was in awe of these trees towering along the curving two-lane highway. The ground was mucky and the flooding was just receding; otherwise we would have visited some of the much bigger trees. Gail showed me how many of the trees have grown out of old stumps.

Mar. 3, 2019. Our reading was on Sunday afternoon at the Iota Press Space / **North Bay Letterpress Arts** in Sebastopol. Pat and Eric Johnson had sent out many announcements and there was a large crowd at the reading. Maureen's brother, Pat, and his wife, Laura, were there; Carol Clavonne (an editor of *Posit: A Journal of Literature and Art*) brought some of her friends from Santa Rosa. One woman who had gone to Bard came to the reading with a stack of my books she had collected over the years. There were many artists present; some who work and show at the letter press studio. The crowd was exceptionally warm and welcoming and they asked deep questions about our writing. We are grateful to Pat Nolan and Eric Johnson for all the pre-work they did to make this event a success, especially since we arrived right after the flood. (Barb)

❀

I was delighted that my brother, Pat, and my sister-in-law, Laura, were able to make it to the reading. I rarely get an opportunity to read with them in the audience. It meant a lot to me to have them there. Eric gets a big "hats off" for his fabulous presses and letterpress type on display and running such a terrific place. Many who came to the reading were artists taking letterpress classes and printing beautiful pieces, several that were on display. He also created two stunning little broadsides of a poem each by us. (MO)

Maureen's brother, Pat, holding books *(MO)*

Pat Nolan introducing *(Barb)*

(MO/Barb)

(Barb)

Bill Vartnaw, Gwynn O'Gara, Nancy Packard *(Barb)*

Gail & Sandy *(Barb)*

I was very happy to finally spend time with Sandy Berrigan. We had written each other in the past and exchanged books, but I had never met her before. We talked about our shared histories with Pat, all three of us growing up in Detroit. Her uncle had owned Sam's clothing store downtown and her mother owned a children's clothing store in the Fisher building at a time when few women worked outside the home. Pat lived in Detroit from the age of thirteen to seventeen; his father was a tool and die maker who relocated them from Pat's birthplace in Montreal to find work in Detroit. Sandy, Pat, and Gail, so good to be with them for these few days—and Nancy, too—I hope our paths cross again (outside of social media and the US post). (Barb)

❄

After the reading, a group of us trooped over to a nearby restaurant that was a holdover from the days of Foster Freeze soft ice cream. The place had actually been a Foster Freeze stand back in the day. I remember as a kid growing up in Monrovia/Duarte that getting a Foster Freeze was a big treat. Nancy offered to buy me a glass of wine to celebrate our last "on-the-road" reading, but I asked for a cone of Foster Freeze instead. It was just as delicious as I remembered it. (MO)

❄

After the reading, a group of us sat around a long wooden table munching on tacos and talking about our lives and projects—Pat and Gail, Jizel Albright, Sandy, Nancy, Barb, and Maureen. Then at home, Pat gave us special paper to copy two of our poems in longhand for Bill Hawley, a collector and a winemaker who traded bottles of wine for our poems. Thanks Bill, we'll think of you when we're home in New York and Denver, drinking your special vintage. Soon after we left Monte Rio, Pat sent us a link to his post about our road trip on his blog, **The Black Bart Poetry Society**. Thank you, Pat. (Barb/MO)

❄

Mar. 4-5, 2019. We set out driving south, adding an extra day to our trip, but thereby avoiding snowy passes on I-80. We planned to drive four hundred miles a day for four days. As we drove along, the hills were a bright lawn green color. Stunning, sloping hills that almost seemed manicured. So green from the rain with black cattle and sheep grazing. Maureen said she had never seen them so green before. Then on I-5 there was one blooming almond orchard after another and orange orchards, the trees heavy hanging down, loaded with fruit. A sign I saw along the road: "Farmers Use Water To Grow Our Food." (Barb)

(Barb)

Finally on March 4th, the last seventy miles; we were on CA-54 heading to Mojave. It was dark before we got to our motel and the GPS told us that we had arrived while we were still on the highway between two dark brown towering mountains with nothing else for miles around. Hum. Maureen called the hotel and they told us which exit to take. Must remember that some addresses should have "Business" in front of their addresses. Business Highway 54.

Then in the hotel room, we started cooking tofu, zucchini, kale, and buckwheat noodles. It's a tight squeeze cooking on a bathroom counter.

113

With my elbow, I knocked the bottle of olive oil and it splattered all over the floor. Dang. How can you make a stir fry without olive oil. Maureen talked the clerk into giving us a handful of butter packs. (Barb)

❈

The next morning when we first left our hotel and started driving through the desert toward the mountains, a vast hillside of the wind turbines appeared spinning wildly in the wind. They created a pattern against the mountain, like a network of giant pinwheels. Finally, just before arriving in Flagstaff, we stopped and washed our car's back window so we could see better. As we got into the mountains by Flagstaff, suddenly our sunny afternoon turned into winter with snow on the mountains. Two more days until Denver and the temperature there today is twenty-four degrees. (MO)

(MO)

(Barb)

Mar. 5- 6, 2019. On the 6th, we loaded our car, got gas, and pulled out of Flagstaff, AZ. A slight drizzle had fallen on the snowy roadsides, but the sky was clearing and the sun was out. Flagstaff's elevation is 6,909 feet above sea level. So chilly, but now we headed out toward a lower elevation and flat desert on I-40 East. The surrounding mountains were fabulous colors in the morning light. The variations of the strata flowed from subtle mauve to rich clay red to purple. The desert floor was sage with bushy yellow clover or mustard scattered in clumps. I felt like I could drive forever under the rolling cumulus, so brilliant white against an ever-lifting blue. As we crossed over into New Mexico the gas stations had enormous stores filled with First Nation turquoise jewelry, woven rugs, handmade moccasins, and a zillion other unique items. I thought of buying my mom some cozy lined moccasins, but getting the right size seemed too tricky. Luckily, we were on a tight schedule to arrive at Santa Fe, so I couldn't drool over the earrings too long. We sped through Albuquerque and arrived at The Sage Hotel in Santa Fe just in time to have a bite at Annapurna's World Vegetarian Café. We didn't have much time to see the sites as we were pretty tired from driving, and the last leg of our Poets on the Road by car would need us up and out early in the morning to arrive in Denver to thank and take over from my mom's caregiver, Jacki, as she was needing to return to Truckee, CA, where she lives. (MO)

❋

As the altitude increased, I started feeling a lack of oxygen. I should have started taking chlorophyll and electrolytes the week before leaving the Bay area. We drove through the mountains and across the flat desert in Arizona, the altitude almost always between four and five thousand feet. For two nights I couldn't sleep, couldn't breathe. In my sleepless state, I kept going back to Brenda Hillman's poems. Suddenly I realized what I needed to do with the project I am working on about my mother: Stand in places where Ferne Hostetter stood or lived in her photographs, and write prose poems. These will be the glue that will hold the project together. (That means more journeys to Detroit.) Sleeplessness pays off sometimes when new ideas surface.

Finally, in Santa Fe at over seven thousand feet, I coaxed myself into sleeping by propping myself up on pillows, taking all my herbs and remedies and reminding myself that one always sleeps with shallow breathing. Instead of giving in to panic, I practiced breathing with shallow breaths and long exhales. Hurray, I fell asleep, and in the morning, I was rested enough to drive. I am very thankful that Maureen did a lot more than half of our driving from Mojave to Denver. (Barb)

(Barb)

We packed our car for the last time in the parking lot of the Sage Hotel. It seemed amazing to think this was it. A day of driving and we'd be in Denver. As I partook of the excellent breakfast in the Sage, the weather report cautioned a day of high hazardous winds. As we drove the wind did indeed pick up. I love to drive, but it took concentration to keep the Honda Fit on the road. A truck pulling a trailer pulled over on the shoulder after bouncing around for several miles ahead of us. The big rigs swayed back and forth as the wind took them. By the time we arrived at Raton Pass, I was a little concerned about navigating the curves at seven thousand and some feet elevation in such fierce gusts. But luck was with us. The wind was quieted some by the pass range, which was a little buffer against it. Also, the pass, which can be a tower of violent weather and low visibility, was sunny! with only scattered snow bits in shaded places. It was the nicest trip through that pass I've ever driven. When we stopped for gas at Trinidad just on the other side of the pass, we got out of the car and almost blew away. The winds followed us to Colorado Springs and then let up slowly. Then traffic began stopping and we saw smoke and that something was burning up ahead. As a highway patrol fellow directed our lane of traffic, we were suddenly right beside a car wildly on fire. I had my camera out, but when confronted by the inferno engulfing the car and starting the ditch grass on fire, I completely forgot about taking a photo. All I could think of was it might explode any second. With the burning car receding in the side mirror, we both hoped the occupants had gotten out safely. (MO)

❀

What do I remember from the trip? As I was dozing off in the car, I took a few photos. The endless mounds of brown hills. Flat land with a dust storm. Wild winds as I ran to a restroom in Arizona; it seemed as if I might blow away or the car door might be ripped off. I hardly remember all the motel rooms we have stayed in, one night after another, beds that hundreds and hundreds of others have slept in. I always wondered, as I wrapped myself in my sheet, how that energy passes between us, from one stranger to the next. (Barb)

(MO)

In Santa Fe, I remembered thirteen years ago living just outside of town in Tesuque. I wrote *Thirty Miles to Rosebud* while living in a barely heated adobe house in the winter. I remember making a quilt while I was there and I sewed it together (on my sewing machine), squares and rectangles of different colors and shapes. It was kind of ragged looking; I always lacked precision in sewing. Later I gave the quilt to my daughter and then it disappeared, probably into the rag heap. While I lived there, I remember a frozen shoulder and driving my car with my arm in a sling in order to shop. I didn't know anyone. Well, there was a young African American artist who lived across the way, and she shopped for me (she worked at Trader Joe's). What an idea to move across country at fifty-seven without knowing a soul. Once I went outside the house (it was on a compound) and there was a bear going through the garbage cans. Not enough time to visit Tesuque, but always enough time for memories. On the road the next morning to Denver. Seven hours and four hundred miles. (Barb)

DENVER
MARCH 7 - 20, 2019

Mar. 7-8, 2019. We arrived in Denver in the thick of rush hour—but got off on a couple of less traveled roads I knew since I live here—and arrived at my back gate. I was really happy to see that gate. As we got close, we phoned my mom's caregiver, Jacki, to meet us outside and take our photo as we stepped out of our car on the Poets on the Road final major stop. Then lots of hugs and happiness to see Jacki and my mom, who has been counting the days to my coming home. (MO)

Photo by Jacki Brennan

We arrived yesterday at Maureen's little bungalow in Denver. Small rooms, lots of photos of family and art, pots and pans, stuffed chairs, a big dining room table, and a small study with a desk and as many books as can fit in the room, floor to ceiling, everywhere. Maureen's mother is ninety-six years old and she wears jeans and a skull cap and leads the way as we go for a walk in the park. I love it when she reaches out with her hands to hold mine. How lucky to have a mother for almost your whole life, especially a mother like Maureen's: De is sweet and tough, and like Maureen, tending toward the affirmative. (Barb)

❁

Total miles that we travelled together in Barbara's 2007 Honda Fit: 5,547 miles. (Barb/MO)

Maureen and De at Harvard Gulch Park *(Barb)*

Jacki leaving Denver to return home to Truckee *(MO)*

If it were not for Jacki Brennan, who stayed with Maureen's mom, and Sarah Morton, who sublet Barbara's apartment, this trip never would have happened. Thanks to both of you. (Barb/MO)

❀

We chilled and rested up for the first week back in Denver. We unpacked the wine we had traded our handwritten poems for in Sebastopol/Monte Rio, sorted books, and I got my paperwork in order for next year's taxes. I reentered the rhythm of taking care of my mom. Then, wanting to celebrate our "We did it!" moment, we organized a little brunch. We had our great California wine from Random Ridge, a 2016 Fortunata red, Barbara's Bill Clinton recipe for quinoa salad, and the amazing, nearby French Trompeau Bakery right down the street. It all came together beautifully with my mom, Junior Burke, Jenny Dorn, Denie Orr, Joanne Weiss, Barbara, and myself around the table. A rollicking crew. It was the perfect toast to our reading adventure! (MO)

❀

I said to Maureen's mother, De: "Before we started our trip, I was mostly alone. On the road, I had to get used to being with Maureen all the time; now I must get used to not being with Maureen." We all laughed.

On my first night here, I dreamed that I was my father, driving his car, and I was myself at the same time. He was going home, finally alive again, but it was me, too, at home, but here I was at Maureen's house. And that night I slept so deeply, finally after lots of restless sleep on the road.

Maureen's mother is fragile, tiny and agile. She climbs the stairs and goes for walks. Her hair is snow white and her eyes are hazel, a little blurry from aging. She is about the age my mother would be if she had lived, rather than dying at thirty-seven. De never smoked and she was physically active her whole life. She had three children, was born on a farm, drove a tractor, worked at many jobs, including at the racetrack, riding and walking the racehorses after a race to cool them out and stretch their legs. Quite a life she has had, growing up without electricity, telephones, running water, cars, and now living in our tech age in Denver. She looks into my eyes and tells me all about how the town where she has lived for the last thirty years, Truckee, CA, in the Sierras has changed. I enjoy watching her and Maureen dozing in the living room and making dinner together. (Barb)

Mar. 16, 2019. At the brunch today, it was great to give **Junior Burke** a big hug. When I was teaching in the low-residence MFA program at Naropa, Junior was in charge of the program and we had lots of phone calls. He has a new novel that I'm looking forward to reading, *A Thousand Eyes.* While the group ate lunch, we talked about our writing projects, our cars, politics, the floods and fires, people we knew, our reading trip, etc. When I talked about my journey working carnivals in the South," Junior told us how he had worked in a carnival too, running a game. It was great to meet up with Jenny Dunbar Dorn again and friends of Maureen's, Joanne and Denie, who had owned a literary bookstore in Denver. (Barb)

Denie, Joanne, Jenny, Junior, Barbara, De *(MO)*

MO and Denie Orr *(Barb)*

Mar. 18, 2019. We met **Steve Katz** and **Jane Wodening**, both long-time friends of Maureen's, at Angelo's Taverna, an Italian restaurant in Denver. I also have known Steve for several years and was happy to meet Jane. Steve brought along a book he had just received from Roberta Neiman of her black and white photographs, *The Magnetic North: Summers with Extraordinary People*, and text from when she, Steve, and his family, as well as other artists and musicians, summered regularly in Cape Breton Island, Nova Scotia. The photos celebrated Robert Frank, JoAnne Akalaitis and the Mabou Mines Troup, Joan Jonas, Philip Glass, Steve, their children and families, and others building their own living shelters in the then wild hills. We passed the book around, looking at the photos while Steve told tales about their many summers there. (Barb)

❋

Barbara talked with Jane about Jane's book, *The Lady Orangutan and Other Stories,* especially one story that Barbara liked a lot, "Of the Unknown," a story about when Jane and Stan Brakhage and their first baby were traveling and living in a station wagon, taking back roads across country. It was a frightening story of unbearable hot weather, an undependable car, wilderness, and a severe cop, so frightening that Jane said she was frightened just writing it.

    After eating pizza and salads, in the parking lot, we said our goodbyes (for now). (MO)

Steve Katz and MO *(Barb)*

Jane Wodening *(Barb)*

Jane, Barbara, Steve, Maureen

Mar. 19, 2019. We had our last reading for this trip at the Mercury Café for the *F Bomb Series*. It was a crowded room; we were happy when Jane Wodening joined us at our table.

Leah Rogin-Roper introduced us. She talked about how she, Nancy Stohlman, Kona Morris, and others were in Barbara's MFA class on flash fiction at Naropa, and how a group of students from that class started their magazine and press, **Fast Forward**, and that was also how this reading series began. The event started with three open readings, one by Kona Morris (a past student of Maureen's, too); she read a short-short story she had written using one of Barbara's prompts.

Our featured co-reader Crisosto Apache read his poems; he is the author of ~~GENESIS~~. Then we read our short-short stories, trading back and forth. Maureen read earlier stories from *Hearts in Space*, and Barbara read from her novel, and also from *Cities & Memory, A Swift Passage*, and newer work. This event was perfect for bringing our on-the-road trip to its final ending, in a carnivalesque room with wall paintings, lush multi-colored draperies, and twinkling lights. (Barb/MO)

Barb, MO, and Collin

(Barb)

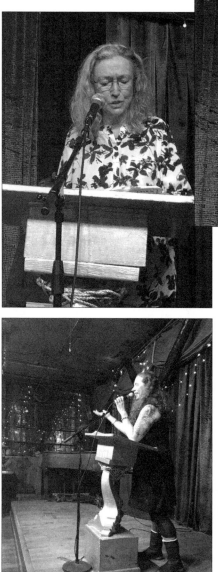

Maureen
Barb
Kona *(Barb)*
Crisosto Apache *(MO)*

Collin Schuster came up after we read with his long-treasured copy of *Hearts in Space* for Maureen to sign. Collin is the publisher of ***Positive Magnets***, an exciting new zine. Later he joined us for a bite to eat and conversation in another restaurant section of the Mercury. (Barb/MO)

At home, we finished our last blog post, the end of our two-month odyssey; in the morning Barbara packed up and headed back to New York, with a one-week stop in Kalamazoo/Detroit. (Barb/MO)

Mar. 20, 2019. A few days after Barbara was back in Brooklyn, Collin Schuster sent us an email with a poem, a fitting end to the trip.

Dear Maureen and Barbara,

It was sweet to meet up with you last night! Thanks for the company.

Most Best,
Collin

AT MERCURY CAFE "IRRESISTIBLE WAVES"

I was carrying the stone of
Posidippus in my pocket
but I lost track of it
in the aisle of swans
(books) (The Prince and the Pea)
(Lowriders in Space) I'm lost in space
(Hearts in Space)
(Barbara and Maureen)
tell me more about the visible sun
and about your friends
the seed lasers generate
over there by the park benches
where the kid chess champions
swap rooks
I've unasked questions
like how to condense the hour into a sky river
to know about D.G. Wills
(Only Lovers Left Alive) Detroit
places you've seen
meeting w/ Diane
and conversations with Bobbie

you're all gracious diamond minds
you'll get to New Orleans
and radiant brown eyes of mesas
the tools of the Mesozoic
when St. Paddy's Day saps clouds
when you condense the steam
it releases Charlie Musselwhite Energy
the biography on Houdini is being held
I thought we lost it but we didn't
we charged the boom box upstairs
"You my all-night study, and you my
midnight, my midnight green"
Telephone Woodland Pattern India
Karen Uhlenbeck wins the Abel Prize
eat your heart out Posidippus!

3/19/2019

Appendix A

Poets on the Road
Pamphlet

Acknowledgments

Barbara Henning

These poems have appeared in *The Brooklyn Rail*, *Journal for Poetics Research*, *Califragile*, *Posit*, *Live Mag!*, *Rascal*, *Talisman*, *Dispatches*, and *The Hurricane Review*. The complete collection, *Digigram*, was published by United Artists in 2020.

Maureen Owen

These poems have appeared in *Dispatches*, *Hanging Loose*, *The Denver Quarterly*, *Positive Magnets*, *The Hurricane Review*, and *Resist Much/Obey Little*. Some will reappear in *let the heart hold down the breakage Or the caregiver's log* (Hanging Loose Press, 2022 and in *everything turns on a delicate measure* (Talisman House, forthcoming).

MAUREEN OWEN

Mom

She wears my flip flops
In midafternoon sun
I shade her ankles & feet
with my shadow

the pines nap too
still & drowsy   in their altitude
as a baby breathes   soft &
scarcely
it hurts my neck but I can't stop
staring up at them   their
glassy needle tops bristle   rolling   heaving
sea above

August 2018

Dazzle Camouflage

Green that goes straight up   tousled locks of branches
then green as still as baize   firs and pines
the great green cargo of these branches   in layers   thick
green hunks of rafts   of forest   pitch and foam

kids across the way put up a makeshift stand
by the side   of the road   shake dust from
little trucks & chant   "Toys
for Sale!"   they plan to buy ice cream with the money

placing cloth chairs in the sun for her   moving to dappled
shade   when sun too hot   then back to sun when shade too cool
try to find a level spot for her chair in slantedness
move small table for water with chair   keep moving as sun
moves   tall shadows of the pines

screeching Steller jays   Dark-eyed junco

no summer insects sing not one   utter silence breaches

it's the last of the 8th Giants up &   leading 3 to 1

Pentecost

I first saw the word
Facsimile   on the nameplate
of a racehorse's halter   a deep
chestnut gelding   I a kid standing
in the shed row   midafternoon sun setting
his coat a red orange fire   he leaning from
his stall door

Her fingers were like little green lizards

except for a lowercase r   rain had washed the ink off the note
fringed as hastily torn paper   encountering a leaf   a
neighbor goes into the grey stucco on the other side of the white
stucco   where wild cactus grows   never let me say
three bare boys stand   a stripped strip of ribbon   chartreuse
plaster   jet   rojo   forest moss   fluttering across genitals

shirts strung
in witty dyes   fold round his shoulders

button down button open at the collar
cherry metallic jacket   panted leg
balanced on the heel of sparky ebony loafers   sans socks
a poor boy   dressed for magic   rococo

there was nothing

where I haven't been   since I hadn't gone
for such a long time

or everybody wants to buy your car

swollen   braided   breathing
seascapes   landscapes   bedroom paintings

did I come away   edgy   on the way back
might those even so   not just need

some fabric never noticed
all the while   this uniquely insisting

what you'd guess   but don't expect
we know the names of the mistakes now

tiny fields of view   seem to squeeze the moon
in a snow like bundles of sheets   rolled in cotton
where dancers move their arms through heavy satin

for Ed Friedman

balmy tomorrow
saturday more snow predicted
the lilacs are in turmoil

or lariat

"All of those years here are gone," she said in Spanish
as she picked through the wreckage littering the trailer
where she and her husband and their five children   had
lived for almost a decade

the way it looked

butter moon   in battered shards   one fourth up the east wall
of the beauty parlor
much as honeycomb that face

that moon squinting   out along
such a sing of cricket katydid hopper
& cicada   loose
stitches in the seam

Chanel referred to the nuns at the orphanage   as her "aunts"
through the glassless windows

on Saturn diamonds rain   down
as into a pool lit from below
whether we were different   fissures

downhill to us   came
a kimono woman swinging   a bright Japanese
lantern   igniting tufts of grass

like a child I have
checked   my closet
before bed

Was death   ever
so beautiful   with
carefully drawn wings
In a long black sheath
an orange yellow lantern
fan in her hand

unbearably slow the Vortex   aviates their arrival

that's just one of the reasons filming birds is frustrating

When you leave someone   you said
to yourself in the elevator going down
the folds and creases of a shirt   the threads and
buttons rushing past
the instant making such economic noise
a tipping solace   awkward if you're   on your own

when you leave someone
you said so yourself in the elevator going down
here's what you should   do
borrowings chipped in haste   adumbrating a plum ferocity
Was that for being too chic   too steep for angling
Perched on a painted result   of   things

at some point you will know   artifact   how we are the result of
what we do to our nature   But it being summer when you
came down
in the elevator   the grass   was sizzling

Liquitex my darling   Fatty acid bloom my love
white haze   newsprint and wax paper   saying   it still does

Or
except various tho she headed

Must we die   Mesopotamia
clocks set right   but the time is wrong

You can help me tie your shoe for you
a little crystal blister   found in a grain field

My mother dreamt of the wind   the ponies
drifting up into the thick dust draft of it

Tiny rectangular forms with legs rushing
about in an ocher glaze

rolls of crepe twisting in manes & tails
wild eyed for oxygen & water

We bring our own territory   with us
terra cotta louche and long it's dawn now taken

we pose   clad uniquely

fungible
     the window   behind us

BARBARA HENNING

The Moon

—hang a dress—in the lobby—wrong size—for 2016—once twirled around—like a flower—on a highway—soon on a hanger—in some other closet—reading Walter Benjamin—*Berlin Childhood*—what was and what might be—a shelter—the rhythm of the railway—ringing of a bell—a butterfly hovering—each passing moment—to gaze—to touch—as a child—the moon—out a Berlin window—*High above the horizon*—then a pale circle—in the afternoon sky—growing growing growing—until it sucks up—tears apart—people place—iron rails—like Krishna opening the veil—*it was my farewell*—Benjamin writes—"*O star and flower, spirit and dress, love, grief, time and eternity!*"—In 1938—this miniature deleted—perhaps, too much—the melancholic grip—start over—at the beginning—with children—the weight of the book—pressing against my chest—drift off— *I collected what I wanted to take across*—he writes—from then to now—

(13 Mar 2016)

On the Q

—to Manhattan—through the slit—between my eyelids—an almost empty car—two women dozing—one leans forward—hair cropped—ear level—mid sixties—freckles—arms crossed—head bobbing—as the train jerks—"little brown bag"—on her lap—the other woman—one leg crossed—over the other—shoulder length—glistening black hair—leaning to the side—head against rail—dozing—trading relatively quiet today—investors returning—from Thanksgiving vacation—the car quiet—climbs over—the Manhattan bridge—behind the ropes and rails—the Brooklyn Bridge—dark scattered clouds—the western sun—a golden hue—a six foot three inch—Justinian cross—over the World Trade center—young adults—brought here as children—soon sent—to places they never knew—underground we go—the conductor says—this is Canal Street—Chinatown—the older woman—stands up—head still bowed—doors open—and then she's gone—

(28 Nov 2016)

String Ball

for Nevine Michaan and Charles Blow

—*the body's organized*—*on a square*—so says Yogi Nevine—I walk around Tompkins Square—all four corners—surely this is the center—of the universe—*the goal in life*—*should be joy*—in Larung Gar—the Chinese—are tearing apart—Tibetan monastic—dwellings—*plan your life*—*like a chess game*—*move analytically*—*with intent*—it's *very practical*—*the way to attain joy*—even for civilians—trapped in Aleppo—with artillery shelling overhead—*defeat in life*—*is bitterness*—buck up—writes Charles Blow—it's over—the bully's—in the white house—for the time being—alt-right is not—a computer command—they're a batch of fanatical racists—*if you're happy*—*you'll help everyone*—*if you're miserable*—*you won't help anyone*—in Shuafat—a refugee camp—in Jerusalem—Baha helps the orphans—work, find direction, survive—then a drive-by—ten bullets—one of the children—will surely—take his place—you can follow—fake news sites—from one to another—unravel the molecular structure—of ribosomes—a tangled mess of rubber bands—and coiled wires—a new pattern—of income equality—life expectancy in the US—declines slightly—*be careful*—*it's like a string ball*—*if we keep going around*—*in the same direction*—*we will surely unravel*—

(1 Dec 2016)

Me, Too

—rheumatic fever—turns the skin—yellow—a heart, scarred——
soon—my mother says—you will—take my place—I wear her old
stockings—dye my hair henna—like hers—smoke cigarettes—wear red
lipstick—her fringed leather jacket—at 18—at the sewing machine—my
foot is hers—pressing the pedal—there's a murmur—in your heart—the
doctor says—but soon it will heal—in the afternoon—I birth a child—
walk down the hallway—in her turquoise bathrobe—at the zoo—an old
female orangutan—locks eyes—with a young woman—breastfeeding a
baby—yes, she nods, *me, too*—at 37—my two children sound asleep—
and all of a sudden—I wake up—surprised to be alive—what about—the
others—I think—the motherless migrants—the refugees—the cumulative
wound—rooms—that murmur—and whisper—remember me—take
care of them—take care of you—

(20 May 2017)

Tompkins Square

—on location—the Grateful Dead's—first East Coast show—
Prabhupada's first US kirtan—chanting and dancing—a rebellious
artifact—or ultimate destination—to blow a trumpet—bang on
some buckets—if I had money—I'd buy a tiny apartment—across
the street—a comeback with millennials—a micro machine—with its
own heartbeat—trying to find a dot—in the pacific—Amelia Earhart
disappears—upward—an old stately elm—leans toward me—then
the voluminous sound—of branches cracking—soon this tree will be
gone—In Mosul—Isis leaves behind—blurred Disney figures—and piles
of—religious rubble—gone like—the birdhouse tree—the men now
say—they'll let women—make birdhouses—to my left—a guy dozing—
on a park bench—a tropical print short-sleeved—button-down—100
percent rayon—a lovely shade of blue—the ultra-rich have great views—
but trees do poorly—in the shade—I, on the other hand—love sitting
here—under the Krishna tree—eating chocolate—and looking—across
the street—at my old apartment—

(12 July 2017)

Now and Again

—to cover misdeeds—puff yourself up—with exaggeration and falsification—your allies—a glittering who's who—in the corporate financial world—supporters—homegrown—Detroit Right Wings—the eighth letter—their icon—88 HH for Heil Hitler—nonetheless—here we are—moving along—as usual—on the train—an old woman—late 80s—her hands shaking—thin—wearing a baseball hat—every human body—a marker in time—a squat woman—body like a boxer—red dyed—ear length hair—unwinds a long—snaking bracelet—carefully reorders—then rewinds—glittering diamonds—on the 6 uptown—a skinny guy—grey messy hair—tiny rimless glasses—tattered jeans and shirt—reading a book—many paper markers—what is it?—lean left—catch "Benjamin"—lean further—"lter"—*Walter Benjamin*—every human body—a marker—to escape Nazis—he took—an overdose of morphine—1940—at 51st street—I stand up—have you read *Berlin Childhood?*—I ask—*yes*—and he likes it too—my favorite Benjamin— did you read the early version—the one—about the moon—*I will*—he says—we nod—then off the train—walking east—just as—the moon crosses over the sun—the city in darkness—for a fleeting moment—

(21 Aug 2017)

Private Eye

—new lessons for cab drivers—in Karachi—don't look at a woman—
in your rear view mirror—don't say anything—about her clothes—
don't ask—if she's married—the exact words—of rickshaw drivers—in
Mysore—to a younger me—now through a green tunnel—of trees on
12th street—I walk to the car—turn on the radio—69 and my eyesight
a little blurry—what to do— —an 18 year old girl—testifies—
the detective's partner watched—in the rear view mirror—guilty of
wearing—a nipple ring—then his turn—keep your mouth shut—they
said—in the women's bathroom—my head hurts—coughing so hard—I
could burst—a brain vessel—Nick Buoniconti'll donate—his brain—to
science—they buy and sell—footballers—the brains typically—come
by FedEx—Dr. Vogel expects Paddock's brain—any day—why did he—
shoot—all those people—Robert E. Lee—says General Kelly—was
honorable—men and women—of good faith—*on both sides*—even
those—who owned and sold human lives—as hedge funds—monetized—
securitized—leveraged—multiple times—then a good cotton and sugar
season—in 1837—the banks collapsed—don't say a word—shut your
mouth—a tax cut—millions of dollars—for the most privileged—I slam
on the brakes—and just miss—a cyclist swerving—into his cell phone—

(6 Nov 2017)

Chocolate

—the dog whines—thumps her tail—pajamas—bare feet—tiptoe down stairs—in the frig—nothing sweet—no left over pudding—scurry up—on the counter—quietly—into the cupboard—a box of cooking chocolate—police officers—lie in wait—nabbing—the child—who sneaks—under the turnstile—unwrap a square—take a bite—uck!—put it back—into the wrapper—into the box—who took a bite?—who did it?—not me—not me—why so skinny—second helpings—for the well fed—a lesson well learned—early on—when they blow a whistle—we scurry to our feet—slam into each other—enough—is enough—why lavish a bully—with the acclaim—so clearly—he demands—the forgotten white majority—where are we going—our young lithe bodies—deep inside—these flesh bags—heart throbbing—climb down—to get away—years later—here alone—in the dark—me, me, me—throbbing—oh so loudly—

(20 Feb 2018)

With a Bang

—with a bang—the hairy flower wild petunia—flings its tiny seeds—sudden and far—how and why—the scientist—kneels down—clamps a metal band—on a pigeon's leg—her initials—and id number—my broken toe—x-rayed, recorded—at the Bleecker Street station—an old man—with head bowed—kneeling—on cardboard—an over-crowded—shopping cart, a sign—*repent*—*the end is near*—the Indian guru whispers—the only sin—to harm oneself—to harm another—is to harm oneself—to repent too much—is to harm oneself—on the platform—the next generation—leans over a keyboard—riffs, breaks, runs—his body hunched—fingers flying—30 miles an hour—all at once—released—the seeds spin outward—the bird flutters into the air—

(18 Mar 2018)

Appendix B

Agenda*

Jan 18, 2019, Friday, 7 p.m.
Belladonna Reading / Brooklyn, NYC
Jackson McNally Bookstore
76 N 4th Street
http://belladonnaseries.org/

Jan 20, 2019, Sunday, 3-5 p.m.
"In Your Ear"/ WDC
DC Arts Center
Reading with Terence Winch and Erika Howsare
2438 18th Street, NW
http://www.dcpoetry.com/iye

Jan 26, 2019, Saturday, 5 p.m.
"Free Series"/ Pensacola, Fla.
Pensacola Museum of Art
407 South Jefferson Street
https://pensacolamuseum.org

Jan 27, 2019, Sunday, 2 p.m.
Mobile Botanical Gardens / Mobile, AL
5151 Museum Drive
https://www.mobilebotanicalgardens.org/

Jan 30, 2019, Wednesday, 7:30 p.m.
The Dragonfly: Poetry and Performance / New Orleans
3921 St. Claude Avenue
Megan Burns historical, now closed, reading space.

Feb 2, 2019, Saturday, 7 p.m.
  Malvern Books / Austin, Texas
  Reading with Ashley Smith-Keyfitz
  613 W 29th Street
  https://malvernbooks.com

Feb 7, 2019, Thursday, 6 p.m.
  Bookworks / Albuquerque, NM
  4022 Rio Grande Blvd NW
  https://www.bkwrks.com

Feb 16, 2019, Saturday, 7 p.m.
  POG Reading / Tucson, AZ
  Steinfeld Warehouse
  101 W Sixth Street
  https://pogartstucson.org

Feb 21, 2019, Thursday, 7 p.m.
  California State University / San Marcos, CA
  The Community and World Series
  Markstein Hall 125
  https://www.csusm.edu/ltwr/news/cwls.html

Feb 22, 2019, Friday, 7 p.m.
  D.G. Wills Bookstore / La Jolla, CA
  7461 Girard Avenue
  http://www.dgwillsbooks.com

Feb 24, 2019, Sunday, 4 p.m.
  Beyond Baroque / Venice, CA
  681 Venice Blvd
  http://www.beyondbaroque.org/calendar.html

Feb 28, 2019, Thursday, Noon
    The Poetry Center
    San Francisco State University
    Steve Dickison's class
    1600 Holloway Avenue
    https://poetry.sfsu.edu

Feb 28, 2019, Thursday, 7 p.m.
    Moe's Bookstore / Berkeley, CA
    2476 Telegraph Avenue
    https://www.moesbooks.com

Mar 3, 2019, Sunday, 3 p.m.
    Iota Press Space / Sebastopol, CA
    North Bay Letterpress Arts
    925D Gravenstein Hwy S
    https://www.iotapress.com

Mar 19, 2019, Tuesday, 7:30 p.m.
    "F Bomb Series" Mercury Café / Denver, Co
    Reading with Crisosto Apache
    2199 California Street
    https://fbombdenver.com

*Links in this section are to the general websites for the bookstores or reading series. Announcements are included in the blog as images or under the "Appendix C: Other Links." All links were working at the time of publication.

Appendix C
Other Links

29   **Lindsey Hanahan**: https://www.amazon.com/Slowing-Down-Light-Lindsey-Hannahan/dp/0942544072

31   **David [Leonard] and Roselyn [Lionheart]**: The link we quoted in the blog no longer has a post for them [http://multiracialmedia.com]. This is their current website: http://www.pangaea.to/daro/index.html

35   **Maurice Carlos Ruffin**: https://www.penguinrandomhouse.com/authors/2156863/maurice-carlos-ruffin/

38   **Megan Burns**: https://jacket2.org/content/megan-burns

39   **Bill Lavender, *Lavender Ink* and *Dialogos*:** https://www.lavenderink.org/site/author/bill/?v=76cb0a18730b

41   **John Hartigan**: https://liberalarts.utexas.edu/anthropology/faculty/hartigan

43   **Ashley Smith-Keyfitz's Malvern Reading**: https://www.youtube.com/watch?v=Qtt3eJmbqrQ

44   **Michael Anania**: https://www.poetryfoundation.org/poets/michael-anania

44   **Maureen Owen's Malvern Reading**: https://www.youtube.com/watch?v=AA3e70b0bkc

44   **Barbara Henning's Malvern Reading**: https://www.youtube.com/watch?v=acQleAv3iGk

54   **Owen/Henning Reading Announcement for Bookworks in Austin**: https://www.bkwrks.com/owen-henning/

53   **Margaret Randall:** http://www.margaretrandall.org

53   **Barbara Byers:** http://www.barbarabyers-books.net

103   **Announcement Berkeley Henning/Owen reading at Moe's Bookstore:** https://www.moesbooks.com/pages/events/26/poetry-flash-presents-barbara-henning-and-maureen-owen

103   *Poetry Flash*: https://poetryflash.org

105   **Gloria Frym**: https://portal.cca.edu/people/gfrym/

108   **Pat Nolan:** https://theoffendingadam.com/author/patnolan/

108   **North Bay Letterpress Arts:** https://www.northbayletterpressarts.org

112   **Pat Nolan's Blog Post on Owen/Henning Road Trip:** https://thenewblackbartpoetrysociety.wordpress.com/2019/03/31/into-the-heart-of-wetness/

122   **Junior Burke:** https://chicagoreader.com/music/musical-and-literary-polymath-thom-bishop-has-a-second-career-as-junior-burke/

122   **Junior Burke's *A Thousand Eyes*** (Winchester Press, UK). https://www.amazon.com/Junior-Burke/e/B07DM6ZTDF%3Fref=dbs_a_mng_rwt_scns_share

124   **Steve Katz:** https://biography.jrank.org/pages/4491/Katz-Steve.html

124   **Jane Wodening:** *https://janewodening.com*

126   **Fast Forward Press:** https://fastforwardflash.wordpress.com/about/

129   *Positive Magnets:* https://livemag.org/issue_16/collin-schuster/

AUTHOR BIOS

Born in Detroit in 1948, **BARBARA HENNING** moved to New York City with her two children in 1984. After a few interim years in Tucson and Mysore, India, she returned to New York in 2010. Presently she's living in Brooklyn. Her most recent book is *Ferne, a Detroit Story*, a hybrid biography of her mother (Spuyten Duyvil, 2022). Barbara is a poet and a fiction writer. She has eight collections of poetry: *Digigram* (United Artists Books), *A Day Like Today* (Negative Capability), *A Swift Passage* (Quale Press), *Cities & Memory* (Chax Press), *My Autobiography* (UAB), *Detective Sentences* (SD), *Love Makes Thinking Dark* (UAB), and *Smoking in the Twilight Bar* (UAB); as well as four novels: *Just Like That* (SD), *Black Lace* (SD), *You Me and the Insects* (SD), and *Thirty Miles to Rosebud* (BlazeVox). She is also the editor of *The Selected Prose of Bobbie Louise Hawkins* (BV), *Looking Up Harryette Mullen* (Belladonna Series), the editor/writer of *Prompt Book: Experiments for Writing Poetry and Fiction* (SD, 2021), and editor/publisher of the poetry/art journal, *Long News: In the Short Century* (1990-1995). She has taught for MFA programs at Naropa University (2006-2014) and Long Island University where she is Professor Emerita. She presently teaches for writers.com. Her readings are on Penn Sound; more information available on her website www.barbarahenning.com

MAUREEN OWEN, former editor-in-chief of *Telephone Magazine* and Telephone Books, currently lives in Denver, Colorado. She is the author of twelve books of poetry, most recently, *let the heart hold down the breakage or the caregiver's log* from Hanging Loose Press and *Edges of Water* from Chax Press. Her title *Erosion's Pull* from Coffee House Press was a finalist for the Colorado Book Award and the Balcones Poetry Prize. Her collection *American Rush: Selected Poems* was a finalist for the *L.A. Times* Book Prize and her work *AE (Amelia Earhart)* was a recipient of the prestigious Before Columbus American Book Award. Other books include *Imaginary Income, Zombie Notes, a brass choir approaches the burial ground, The No-Travels Journal,* and *Untapped Maps.* She has most recently published work in *Three Fold, Dispatches, Positive Magnets, Hurricane Review, The Denver Quarterly, Blazing Stadium, The Brooklyn Rail,* and *Posit.* An instructor of numerous workshops and classes in poetry and book production, her awards include grants from the Foundation for Contemporary Arts, the Fund for Poetry, and a Poetry Fellowship from the National Endowment for the Arts. She has taught at Naropa University, both on campus and in the low-residency MFA Creative Writing Program, and served as editor-in-chief of Naropa's online zine *not enough night.* She can be found reading her work on the Penn Sound website.